DISCOVERING THE CHURCH

LIBRARY OF LIVING FAITH

JOHN M. MULDER, General Editor

DISCOVERING
THE CHURCH

BY
BARBARA BROWN ZIKMUND

THE WESTMINSTER PRESS
PHILADELPHIA

BOOK DESIGN BY DOROTHY ALDEN SMITH

First edition

Published by The Westminster Press®
Philadelphia, Pennsylvania

PRINTED IN THE UNITED STATES OF AMERICA
9 8 7 6 5 4 3 2 1

Library of Congress Cataloging in Publication Data

Zikmund, Barbara Brown.
  Discovering the church.

  (Library of living faith)
  Bibliography: p.
  1. Church. I. Title. II. Series.
  BV600.2.Z54 1983   262   82-23870
  ISBN 0-664-24441-6 (pbk.)

CONTENTS

FOREWORD

The word "theology" comes from two Greek words—
theos ("God") and *logos* ("word" or "thought"). Theology is simply words about God or thinking about God. But
for many Christians, theology is remote, abstract, baf-
fling, confusing, and boring. They turn it over to the
professionals—the theologians—who can ponder and in-
quire into the ways of God with the world.

This series, Library of Living Faith, is for those Christians who thought theology wasn't for them. It is a
collection of ten books on crucial doctrines or issues in
the Christian faith today. Each book attempts to show
why our theology—our thoughts about God—matters in
what we do and say as Christians. The series is an
invitation to readers to become theologians themselves—
to reflect on the Bible and on the history of the church
and to find their own ways of understanding the grace of
God in Jesus Christ.

The Library of Living Faith is in the tradition of
another series published by Westminster Press in the
1950s, the Layman's Theological Library. This new collection of volumes tries to serve the church in the
challenges of the closing decades of this century.

The ten books are based on the affirmation of the
Letter to the Ephesians (4:4–6): "There is one body and
one Spirit, just as you were called to the one hope that
belongs to your call, one Lord, one faith, one baptism,
one God and Father of us all, who is above all and
through all and in all." Each book addresses a particular
theme as part of the Christian faith as a whole; each book
speaks to the church as a whole. Theology is too important to be left only to the theologians; it is the work and
witness of the entire people of God.

But, as Ephesians says, "grace was given to each of us
according to the measure of Christ's gift" (Eph. 4:7), and
the Library of Living Faith tries to demonstrate the
diversity of theology in the church today. Differences, of
course, are not unique to American Christianity. One
only needs to look at the New Testament and the early
church to see how "the measure of Christ's gift" produced disagreement and conflict as well as a rich variety
of understandings of Christian faith and discipleship. In
the midst of the unity of the faith, there has never been
uniformity. The authors in this series have their own
points of view, and readers may argue along the way with
the authors' interpretations. But each book presents
varying points of view and shows what difference it
makes to take a particular theological position. Sparks
may fly, but the result, we hope, will be a renewed vision
of what it means to be a Christian exhibiting in the world
today a living faith.

These books are also intended to be a library—a set of
books that should be read together. Of course, not everything is included. As the Gospel of John puts it, "There
are also many other things which Jesus did; were every
one of them to be written I suppose that the world itself
could not contain the books that would be written" (John

21:25). Readers should not be content to read just the volume on Jesus Christ or on God or on the Holy Spirit and leave out those on the church or on the Christian life or on Christianity's relationship with other faiths. For we are called to one faith with many parts.

The volumes are also designed to be read by groups of people. Writing may be a lonely task, but the literature of the church was never intended for individuals alone. It is for the entire body of Christ. Through discussion and even debate, the outlines of a living faith can emerge.

Barbara Brown Zikmund is an ordained minister in the United Church of Christ, and she is currently the Dean of the Pacific School of Religion in Berkeley, California. A church historian, Dr. Zikmund served on the faculty of Chicago Theological Seminary before assuming her present post. In this book she looks back on what the church has been, how it appears to people today, and how we might "discover" its richness and promise in the future. "This project has allowed me to draw together my thinking about the church at a time of personal transition and change," she said. "Through family illness and death, through new professional opportunities, I have come to appreciate even more deeply why I love the church. As a newcomer to the western edge of the continental United States, I have a keen sense of anticipation about the future of the church in Asia and other developing areas. As a churchwoman I am angry over the ways the church has ignored or used my sisters past and present, but I am optimistic that God's freedom in Christ can invade the church even more completely in the future. My theology has become more incarnational, and for me this means that the church in its concrete forms is the means of God's grace."

DISCOVERING THE CHURCH is intended to be read with *The Joy of Worship*, by Marianne H. Micks, another volume in the Library of Living Faith, and together they point to new ways in which the people of God can proclaim the good news to a broken world.

JOHN M. MULDER

Louisville Presbyterian Theological Seminary
Louisville, Kentucky

1
WITHIN POPULAR CULTURE

Here is the church,
Here is the steeple,
Open the doors
And see all the people.

When we look at current religious life and practice,
one of the unique things about Americans is that we are a
churchgoing people. For reasons that are sometimes
difficult to explain we have deep commitments to and
involvements in churches. From our colonial beginnings
to contemporary practice, Americans are more likely to
affirm the importance of, or be involved in, the institutional church than many Christians around the world.
And even when people do not consider themselves
believing Christians, they will often defend the importance of the church. Why?

In popular thinking the church is a good thing. People
will disagree as to why, but most folks consider main-
stream religious life and practice important. We have
laws to protect religious freedom, and even when we do
not agree with our neighbors, we will defend their right
to believe what they want and worship as they wish. It is
appropriate, therefore, to begin our consideration of the
church with the popular ideas surrounding the church

11

which pervade our culture. Those of us who are deeply involved in the church are inclined to turn to the Bible, or celebrate the history of the church, but most people in our culture begin with quite practical considerations: Why go to church? Why join a church? Why support any church with one's time and money?

Their answers indicate the following: For some people the church is a keeper of values, for others it is a helpful service organization. Still others look to the church as a place to belong, and some people feel that relating to the church is like buying an insurance policy. Let us look more closely at these popular perspectives on the church.

The Church as Keeper of Values

In contemporary life, which is characterized by high mobility and cultural pluralism, many people fear that basic values are being slowly eroded. Young people do not know what to believe or how to tell right from wrong. Parents have little guidance about how to raise children in this complex world. Newspapers report assassinations and political dishonesty. Public schools are caught trying to cultivate creativity while maintaining discipline. It seems to many that very few places are left in our society where people take a position or stick their necks out. Therefore, in the chaos and confusion of many causes and concerns, the church seems to have an important function. It preaches and teaches the Ten Commandments and the Golden Rule. Even many unchurched persons will agree that the church needs to exist, because it shapes basic values and passes them on from generation to generation. Our entire civilization will suffer if we do not recognize how the church preserves morality and character.

When people are asked why they belong to a church, they respond with words similar to this California father:

> I think one of the biggest and most important things is my children. I definitely want them brought up as Christians, and the Church is obviously the center or the hub for spreading this word, this information, more so than just sitting at home and reading the Bible and trying to interpret it on your own. At church you've got the instructor, the pastor, who can lend meaning to those things that you don't understand. You have the center there to come together with other Christians with similar ideas and obviously the same beliefs. You can talk to people freely about your beliefs and programs and shall we do this and that. (Edward A. Rauff, *Why People Join the Church*, p. 79)

Within the church we recognize that education is basic to our identity. After all, Jesus was a teacher who spent most of his ministry sharing new values in a confusing world very much like our own. He told the first disciples that outward appearances were not as important as inner convictions, that genuine leadership was expressed in service, that loving one's neighbor as oneself was the greatest commandment. Throughout human history, in times of war and political upheaval churches have kept the faith. Church buildings and church leaders have saved art and information to share with future generations. And although this concern for preservation has its limits and problems, church schools and universities have served Western civilization well.

On the American frontier, churches were always viewed as "civilizing institutions." When a preacher came to town to lead a revival, or a local congregation organized itself, the results were literally sobering and enriching. Libraries, schools, welfare services, and social conditions always seemed to improve when the church became involved. We have only to look at the impact of the travels of Pope John Paul II to see the contemporary moral influence of the church. It is out of this tradition that many people still look to churches as "keepers of values."

THE CHURCH AS A HELPFUL SERVICE ORGANIZATION

For other people the church is even more important because of what it actually does to help people. This might be called the pragmatic view of the church. It considers the record. The church works. It not only symbolizes and keeps the best of human values, it acts. It is useful to society. It channels human energies and uses the talents of good people to do good things.

Our voluntary churches have an amazing record. Over and over, churches have sensitized people to problems and moved to become aggressive agents for change. Churches have spread information and met needs. Churches have moved into the unknowns of colonial life, frontier expansion, foreign cultures, urban growth, and social upheaval to improve human life. Christian missionaries have shared the benefits of modern knowledge with many unfortunate peoples. And although we cannot ignore those stories of insensitive cultural imperialism, the great expansion of the church throughout the world in the past several centuries has greatly benefited humankind.

Today, church organizations are major channels for basic food and medical supplies in times of war and natural catastrophe. Church institutions provide shelter and services to orphans, victims of domestic violence and rape, physically and mentally disabled persons, refugees, prisoners of war, and the elderly. Church people have spoken out against racism and sexism. In many situations they have made a political difference.

Although some people will argue that the social pro-

grams of modern governments have nullified the importance of the church as a helpful organization, the argument remains. Church people are committed to serve.
They are not bound by government regulations or dependent upon public legislation. They give their own money
and commit their own time. They are free to act with care
and concern in very effective ways.

And the record is impressive. People who are not sure
what they believe are confident that they want to be part
of the church. It is a good cause. As with many good
causes, a particular individual may not have personal
need of its benefits or services, but it deserves everyone's support. People belong because it is the right thing
to do. The church is a positive force in the world and it
ought to receive the support of decent people. It is a
helpful organization.

The Church as a Place to Belong

Many people value the church as a place to meet
people. Deep friendships are made and maintained in
churches. And although there are other places where
community is nourished, one of the primary reasons that
people seek out the church is to find congenial people
and enjoy their company. One attractive middle-aged
woman said it well:

> I really get a lot out of it. Well, companionship for one
> thing . . . belonging. I think that's very important, especial-
> ly nowadays when you can't even visit your friends without
> a written invitation, because everybody's so wrapped up in
> their own tiny world, and they don't want you butting in.
> So it's very hard to really belong anywhere except to your
> own family. And I think in a church you have a feeling of
> belonging and being with other people that feel the same
> way you do about things. And it's a very nice feeling.
> (Rauff, *Why People Join the Church*, p. 89)

We live in a very complicated world filled with many lonely people. The older structures of community and family are fading. It is hard to know how to meet people. To protect ourselves against crime and violence, we lock our doors and teach our children not to talk to strangers. Because we do not live in one place very long, we do not have natural channels for social engagement. And because we may move on next month or next year, we run out of the energy to make new friends and keep the old.

The church becomes, therefore, a place for modern people to escape from the loneliness and anonymity of their lives. Singles meet other singles. Divorced and widowed people find that they are not unique. Young parents share the tensions of their lives. Children find friends. Seniors develop programs that give new meaning to those retirement years spent miles away from family. Today's churches are filled with programs that encourage meeting and mixing.

Although sometimes belonging to a particular church is part of an image that people manipulate to gain political success or social status, belonging remains a basic human need. The country club church is still made up of people who crave companionship and fight loneliness. In very practical ways the church keeps people happy by providing a place to belong.

THE CHURCH AS AN INSURANCE POLICY

There is an old story that one well-meaning church member in a small-town church had considerable success recruiting new members to join the church by noting: "Our church has a beautiful cemetery, and only members of the church can be buried there. You should be a member of the church in case something happens."

Whether to guarantee a gravesite or to protect against

eternal damnation, some people support the church "just in case." They will quickly tell you that they do not believe the Bible, or go to worship, or accept any of the creedal affirmations of the church. But they keep their membership, baptize their babies, and pay their pledges as an ecclesiastical insurance against the outside possibility that Christianity might be right. They go to church because they ought to. It doesn't hurt. They defend the church because it is prudent.

Yet the church remains basically irrelevant in day-to-day living. At one time in history, there may have been good reasons for the church, but those reasons have long ceased to be convincing. An individual may decide to join the church for historical or artistic reasons, but that is only a matter of taste. Progress, history, science, medicine, psychology, philanthropy, and government have assumed, transformed, explained away, or superseded the many roles and functions once held by the church.

From this perspective the church is harmless and weak. Uneducated and unsophisticated people lean on the church, but strong people do not need it very often. Yet, haunted by the remote possibility that the fate of one's soul could rise or fall with the church, people defend its existence. It is supported because it is their spiritual insurance.

POPULAR CULTURE

The church continues to flourish in American society. Certain denominations or traditions are more popular now than they were in past years, but they will fade as new theologies and practices take their place. The popular image of the church is positive, even if it is taken less seriously than in times past. It thrives on the popular conviction that churches ought to exist as keepers of values, organizations that do good, places to belong to, and sources of religious services or spiritual insurance. It is deeply embedded in what some observers call "the grass-roots mind."

"Grass-roots" is an American colloquialism that describes something "close to, or emerging spontaneously from, a people." It is the "grass-roots mind" that supports the church at the popular level. Although this mentality tends to operate within a narrow and highly personal frame of reference, a knowable and manageable world, it is not totally closed. Furthermore, it has a keen appreciation for the present, not in order to ignore the past or the future, but to celebrate "now" as the most important time. Finally, it changes very slowly.

> It survives the rise and fall of idea systems, of doomsday forecasters, of charismatic personalities, of each new "alienated" generation, and of technological revolutions. . . . While intellectuals embrace the very latest in idea fashions and causes, the grass-roots mind remains anchored in its world of familiar people and familiar axioms. Indeed there is a good bit of cultural support for doing just that. It loves novelty, but wisely rejects it as a way of life. The story of the grass-roots mind is a tale of basic composure in the face of the wrenching influences of the twentieth century. (Conal Furay, *The Grass Roots Mind in America*, pp. 16–17)

This mentality is at the core of American popular culture. It is characterized by an emphasis on individualism, a focus upon traditional values, and genuine optimism about the future. "Popular culture catches people in their most relaxed moments, when they are defenseless, so to speak. It shapes them, or perhaps more exactly, confirms them in the shape that other facets of culture have already created" (Furay, *The Grass Roots Mind in America*, p. 58). Theologians do not like to admit the significance of these perspectives on the church, but they cannot be ignored. Indeed, it might be argued that only when a theology of the church, or ecclesiology, begins to recognize the ways in which average people understand the church will it have an adequate foundation. Biblical, historical, and theological factors aside, we fail to understand something very basic about the church unless we begin with these popular understandings held by many Americans.

2
THROUGH PERSONAL TESTIMONY

Now we've got to find some way of telling them why we'd rather go to church than play softball on Sunday morning. One thing I'd tell them is about this right of mine. It's my right to choose to go to church on Sunday. I also believe it's an educational procedure for myself, because even though I know God, I want to learn more. . . . And I think that sometimes in church I might be able to find somebody else that needs some help from me, and I'd be more than happy to share that. (Rauff, *Why People Join the Church,* p. 162)

Beyond the popular justifications for the church which are generally part of our culture, people appreciate the church for very personal reasons. They have experienced its value. Church is specifically important to them, not just for what it does in general. Church is experienced as "supportive of my life, helping me with my problems, feeding my unique needs, and satisfying me." For many people that is the bottom line. Although what the church does for the larger society is good, ultimately church is a very personal thing.

This perspective is especially important to people who judge that the many centuries of close connection between the important centers of human civilization and the Christian church are coming to an end. In modern history the dominance of Christian institutions and Western modes of thinking (Christendom) cannot be denied. In some respects it has been an incredible success story. But in the late twentieth century only one third of the world's population is even nominally Christian. We are entering a post-Christian era. And because we have linked the gospel to the political fortunes of particular economic and political systems, as they wane in power and influence so does the church. In a sense we are becoming victims of our success.

One common response to this situation is to see the church only in personal terms. People who might wish to value the power of the church as a public guardian of values or a major force for good in the world are scaling down their expectations. When we ask them, "Why relate to the church?" they tell us only personal stories. The church supports them through the ups and downs of life. It offers help in times of crisis and trouble. Belonging to a church is important because it offers special things, opportunities, and community for them. Personally, they need the church, even if its social value can be questioned. With this perspective we might say that the church becomes privatized.

The Church Supports Me Throughout My Life

Anthropologists point out that every human society has certain religious practices and rituals to support the rhythms of daily life from its beginning to its end. Christianity participates in this pattern. Many of the services, rites, and special events in our churches revolve around the movement of human beings from birth to death. Some people think of the church as the place for marrying and burying. They would not feel married without a church wedding, and they would not think of having a family member buried without the blessing of the church. People will ignore the church at other times of their lives, but these things are essential.

Churches have sacraments, ordinances, or ceremonies for most of the important events in a person's life. Infant baptism, or child dedication, marks the beginning of life's journey. Some churches have rituals for blessing women after childbirth. Others have ceremonies for naming. As a baby grows up, programs of Christian nurture and education instill a sense of self-worth and belonging. At certain points along the way, Bibles may be presented and special recognition given.

When a child "comes of age" (variously defined), all churches have special ways to celebrate. For those churches which did not baptize the infant, believer's baptism becomes a time when a young person takes a personal faith stance. Special experiences, studies, preparations, and clothing lead up to ceremonies that may involve total immersion. For young people who were baptized as infants confirmation becomes the important step. After careful preparation, confirmands reaffirm for themselves those vows which their parents took to raise them in the Christian faith. For some churches this step may be associated with a child's first Communion. For others it is literally called the church membership class. Churches spend a great deal of energy on children and youth. All churches attempt to take seriously the admonition that Christians should raise up their children in the ways of the Lord.

> When you are little and ugly somebody carries you in church on a pillow, and you come out a child of God and inheritor of the Kingdom of Heaven. They pour water on your head and that's a sacrament. When you are twelve you walk back in yourself with your best dress and shoes on, and your new prayer book your mother buys you, and you walk up to the Bishop, and he stands up, and you kneel down, and he mashes on your head, and you are an Episcopal. Then you are supposed to increase in spirit. Then everybody kisses you and that's a sacrament. Only I

left out the bread and the wine. That's a sacrament too. I
tasted some of the bread in the choir room and it tasted just
like my gold fish wafers. (Virginia Cary Hudson, *O Ye Jigs
& Juleps!*, pp. 1–2)

For adults the church also provides important support.
It is probably the most obvious in connection with
marriage. When a man and a woman decide to get
married, most of the time they look to the church. Priests
and pastors counsel with the couple and officiate at a
ceremony or sacrament where family and friends can
witness the promises; and where the forming of a new
family unit is recognized before God. In today's world,
churches are often called upon to bless and honor other
adult relationships and commitments. New jobs, new
homes, new obligations, and the responsibilities of lay-
persons in the church are set apart by special services of
promise and thanksgiving.

Many churches set forth moral codes and axioms to
guide their members down to the smallest details of daily
life. What one should eat, or wear, or read is closely
defined by the church. Acceptable ways to use leisure
time and how Christians ought to spend or save money
are carefully outlined. Although most churches do not
monitor daily existence so closely, the assumption that
the church has an important obligation to guide and
support the proper life is fundamental.

Of course when things are not going well, the church
provides assistance also. From ancient practice there is
the expectation that believers will regularly confess their
sins and receive word of God's pardon or assurance
through the church. Some traditions preserve personal
rites of penance; others place this supportive experience
in the context of corporate worship.

The church generally assists members in developing
helpful patterns of private piety and devotion. Prayer
retreats, Lenten programs, pilgrimage centers, stations of

the cross, summer camps, and yearly revival meetings stimulate church members to renew and to keep their faith. At the heart of Christian worship is the sacred meal of bread and wine. The Mass, Communion, Eucharist, Lord's Supper, or Table Service, as it is variously called, offers regular spiritual nourishment to faithful Christians. Many churches also run practical programs for single parents, alcoholics, and recently divorced men and women. When children leave the home and retirement approaches, churches become especially important to the elderly.

Finally, in a society where more and more people are living longer and healthier lives, the churches have a significant ministry to the dying and to those who grieve at times of death. The reality of death and the pain of suffering and loss does not get easy. Churches provide wider perspectives on human existence and promises that God cares. Churches help people to place what is happening to them in a broader context. Although various Christian traditions may understand and proclaim the Easter message quite differently, our resurrection faith does not despair at death. This conviction offers solace to people as the cycle of life draws to its end.

THE CHURCH RESCUES ME IN TIMES OF CRISIS

People turn to the church at all times of personal crisis, not simply at death. Pastors remark that helping persons through difficulties and change is fundamental to the church's ministry. A crisis may be caused by illness, the death of a loved one, a drug overdose, a brush with the law, the loss of a job, a divorce, or some difficult experience or assignment. In periods of personal change and trouble previous values and life-styles are questioned. In some cases a crisis leads to illness and breakdown. In other cases the result is a dramatic conversion. In all cases such events demand a reordering of priorities and values, and a seeking of help to meet new needs. In these times for many people the church becomes an important source of strength.

When church members look back upon periods of crisis, many will say that they were God-given. Sometimes it seems as if the Holy Spirit leads them through failures toward wholeness in the church. One Lutheran man put it this way:

> I became aware of those failures, and so I realized what a heap of nothingness I really was, and that I needed someone other than myself. Different people had shared with me before, but I was still up here somewhere and I hadn't reached the low point. Hadn't been dragged to the bottom of the pit, so to speak. And so God wasn't finished with me. He had to take me through these things—the experience of divorce, the experience of failure in school, failure in jobs, and it was then that I was ripe. I didn't have any place else to turn, and I realized I wasn't really that great. And I could turn to the Lord. (Rauff, *Why People Join the Church*, p. 103)

In Christian history this has been called the "dark night of the soul." It comes when we are vulnerable and weak, when we have been stretched beyond our limits, when our world crumbles around us. In extreme situations we need skilled medical care and therapy. But in the experience of many people the church offers salvation. Because Christian doctrine begins with the assumption that human beings are limited, finite, and flawed (what has been meant by the doctrine of original sin), the church does not ignore even the most deplorable aspects of human nature and experience. Christian theology refuses to perpetuate the myth that if we know the good, we will be able to do the good. It accepts us for what we are, "warts and all," but it does not stop there. The good news, or gospel, is that God knows us completely and provides a way out. We may call it grace, atonement,

redemption, salvation, or being "saved." But whatever
we call it, the message to those in despair is one of hope
for tomorrow.

When we probe deeply into the reasons people participate in churches, there is often a story of crisis and
healing behind their membership. Joining and serving in
the church is not a luxury, but a necessity. In gratitude
for what it has done in the past, or out of a sense of
obligation related to some personal crisis, people who
have been through difficulties give their support to the
church. They appreciate God's work in their lives, and
they know that without the church they would be less.

For those people who have been helped by the church
there is the additional conviction that they must carry on
God's work. They appreciate what has been done; and
they anticipate how the church can help others in the
future. Belonging to the church is an expression of their
personal confidence in Christianity and the church. With
missionary zeal these church members witness to the
world that the church has made a difference in their
lives. They encourage friends to join the church for very
personal reasons. They testify to the fact that the church
has resources to rescue everyone in times of crisis.

The Church Serves My Special Interests

The so-called privatization of the church is emphasized by its significant role in the human life cycle, and
through the meaningful ways it rescues people who
falter. Finally, it centers on those particular special
things the church is, or does, "for me."

Often people will choose a church because of its
leadership. They like the minister or priest. In churches
where preaching plays a large role in worship, the
capacity of the preacher to speak to the hearts and minds
of a congregation is no small matter. Families will drive

miles every week in order to hear the sermons of Reverend X. In some instances devotion to one pastor will cause persons to change membership or increase contributions. "He speaks to me." "She makes the Bible come alive." "He is always so interesting." These are the comments of enthusiastic members who appreciate their church because of its preacher. Devotion to a truly charismatic leader remains the central reason many members support and participate in their churches.

Sometimes a special attachment to a particular church is not as personal, but it is no less powerful. Many people are attracted to a church because of its convenient or picturesque location. It is the place, more than the preacher or the people, that appeals. Maybe there are strong family ties to a certain church; maybe it is a symbolic center in the local town or area. Sometimes people simply join the church that is the closest to home.

Architecture is another reason people will choose one church over another. From Gothic buildings with stained-glass windows to modern steel and concrete structures, churches inspire loyalty. A building is not the church, yet the capacity of a person to worship in a particular space and to sense God's presence in that place is important. When you ask people about their church, many are quick to tell you about the building. It symbolizes God's care and love. It is a personally "holy" place. There is some evidence that the type of building which seems "sacred" to a person is established quite early in childhood. Most people cannot be inspired by something dramatically different from what they knew as "religious" while they were growing up.

When talking about churches we cannot ignore the role of music. Because biblical and theological truth is so difficult to explain in words, and because worship calls upon more than the intellect, music has a central place in Christian worship. Organs, choirs, and congregational singing enrich corporate worship immeasurably. The high mass, or the second service, in many churches is just like other services, except for the music. Among ethnic churches the importance of music to celebrate the particular cultural traditions of a church is recognized. People who wish to sing, to play instruments, or simply to listen to Bach or gospel music will select their church on the basis of the quality and opportunities in its music program. In fact, many people do not care a great deal about the content of worship, as long as the music is "good."

Sometimes people join a church because it provides an important channel for personal commitments to certain issues or principles. For instance, pacifism is a political and moral stance that certain "peace churches" uphold. The complex relationship between church and state, and how we best protect religious freedoms, is something that divides Christians. Because of the general Christian focus upon basic human rights, persons who are working on specific issues of justice and liberation regularly turn to churches to mobilize opinions and generate political action. Hunger, ecology, busing, nuclear arms, abortion, and inclusive language are only a few of the important questions that draw people to or alienate people from certain churches. Most everyone agrees, however, that although the causes (and positions) will vary from church to church, depending upon location and membership, the obligation of churches to wrestle with important social issues is fundamental. Some individuals will join a church because it takes a stand on an issue. Other individuals will quit a church when it does the same thing. This phenomenon only emphasizes the highly personalized ways people justify their church.

Finally, healthy churches have historically been close (and even closed) communities of caring and commitment. In American experience denominations and parishes have emerged along linguistic, racial, economic, and cultural lines. It has been natural and normal for people to seek out people like themselves in church. And churches, therefore, have become very homogeneous institutions. Choosing a church, for many people, becomes an exercise in finding a congregation made up of "my kind of folks."

Interestingly enough, two justifications are given for this highly personalized understanding of authentic church life. On the one hand, there are those who insist that only strong committed congregations which maintain a unique religious stance over against the secular world will be able to survive. On the other hand, it is argued that only when congregations respond to the sociological realities of our world will they be able to survive.

The first perspective emphasizes that institutional strictness, worldly separation, theological conservatism, and evangelical zeal are the marks of a successful congregation. People want a church that specifically affirms their personal faith and interests. Furthermore, churches that exhibit such characteristics grow. Although these criteria do not always correlate with church growth, they do seem to lead to congregational health among people who already feel alienated economically, politically, educationally, psychologically, and spiritually from the centers of power in the world. Minority, immigrant, and less successful persons in our society gravitate toward churches that are more strict, separate, conservative, and evangelical, because they serve their special interests in a world that generally doesn't seem to care. (See Dean M. Kelley, *Why Conservative Churches Are Growing.*)

The other defense of the homogeneous church comes from the church growth movement. Sociologists have looked at the characteristics of congregations that thrive and discovered that they are homogeneous units in stable communities. When communities change racially and economically, churches do not grow because people find it more difficult to locate a church that serves their special interests. The case is made, therefore, that rather than withdrawing from the world, churches that wish to be successful need to tailor themselves to the social context. This might mean leaving some areas and moving into other areas. By rejecting "people blindness" (that is, the tendency of churches to ignore the significant cultural differences that separate people into groups), churches can maximize the chances that growth and stability will occur. When congregations with adequate programming move to identify and contact just those persons who can be predicted to be the most receptive to a particular church (because they are similar in values, culture, background, and religious expectations), they flourish. The advocates of this approach are simply building upon the reality that people select their church for very personal reasons. (See C. Peter Wagner, *Your Church Can Grow.*)

From a theological standpoint both of these arguments present difficulties. Yet before we discount them completely, it is important to recognize their grounding in reality. People do appreciate and join churches that serve their special interests, their people, their life-style, their needs, and their faith. What is so wrong about that?

In our highly pluralistic world this is a crucial question for the churches. Many ethnic and racial groups do not want to discount the value of homogeneity in their churches. The church is important as the preserver and nurturer of special traditions and subcultures. If the church does not do this, minority heritages will be absorbed into the dominant culture and lost forever. Minority people will lose an important resource for shaping and supporting ethnic identity. As a people who take history seriously and draw strength from the past, they argue that Christians need to encourage certain kinds of homogeneity.

The black church is a good case in point. The capacity of Afro-Americans to understand themselves and participate fully in our society is supported by a strong black church. If we ignored the need for these churches and advocated a situation in which all churches moved toward a racial mix proportional to the numbers of blacks in the population at large, no one would be happy. It would not work and such an interracial super church would not appeal to many people.

Yet, what are we to do? Carl Dudley believes that an acceptance of this perspective on the church may be

> a judgement upon the church's failure to embrace as Christ's family "all people who come in the name of the Lord." The body of Christ is not predetermined by the exterior similarity of social class and cultural background. The people of God are not simply the fractured reflections of divisions that exist on earth. The very effectiveness of the homogeneous principle is, according to church theology, both catholic and reformed, a denial of the fullness of Christ at any given time and place on earth. (Carl Dudley, *Where Have All Our People Gone?*, p. 57)

He may be right, but the perspective expressed by Dudley is not that of popular culture or personal appreciation. It draws upon biblical and theological understandings of the church. It distinguishes between what the church is and what it ought to be, or what it is called by God to be. Thus far we have examined the church only from the perspective of human experience and contemporary practice. Now it is time to consider the church from other perspectives.

3
WITHIN BIBLICAL AND THEOLOGICAL TRADITIONS

When therefore we say that we believe in the church, we do so only and always in terms of our belief in the God who judges and raised up. The mistake of ecclesiasticism through the ages has been to believe in the Church as a kind of thing-in-itself. The apostles never regarded the Church as a thing-in-itself. Their faith was in God, who had raised Jesus from the dead, and they knew the power of his resurrection to be at work in them and their fellow-believers despite the unworthiness of them all. (A. M. Ramsey and Leon-Joseph Suenens, *The Future of the Christian Church*, p. 38)

The church viewed from biblical and theological traditions moves beyond popular and personal perspectives to insist that the church is more than our human experience or effort. The church is holy or divine. It is God's. We can never create the church, we receive it as a gift. Furthermore, although most Christians say that they believe in the church, the church itself never becomes the object of faith or worship. It exists because God's gracious love for humanity found ultimate expression in the life, death, and resurrection of Jesus Christ. When human beings open themselves to the "new life" offered by faith through the Christ, they are the church. They

32

participate in a community that belongs to God from the beginning of all time.

To be part of the church is multidimensional. It is a very human institution, as we have already seen. From the biblical and historical perspective, however, it is much more than a human organization. It may consist of buildings and programs, but fundamentally it is made up of Christians in response to God. Church members have special gifts and obligations, but all are bound together in the biblical metaphors of one "people," one "body," and one "Spirit." The church exists authentically in each local parish and in every place and time. It is universal. The part is equal to the whole, because each part possesses, not a fragment of Christ, but the whole Christ. Thus, a local church is a complete church in that place. And finally, the church is a living vehicle for Christ's ongoing presence and ministry. It does not exist as a memorial society or a keeper of traditions. Rather, it celebrates the vitality of the Christian life and anticipates a tomorrow where God's will shall be done on earth as it is in heaven.

What does it mean to view the church in this way? Although many of the phrases used above are familiar to churchgoing people, it is never a simple task to explain biblical and theological statements about the church. If we want to move beyond the popular and personal perspectives, however, it is important to try. We begin with the word "church."

THE "CHURCH"

In English, the word "church" is used in many ways. It describes a building in which Christian people meet for worship. It refers to the organizations, denominations, or communions that members affiliate with when they join a local congregation. It means the clerical and priestly

leadership of certain parts of the Christian community. It
defines the worldwide fellowship of those who follow
Jesus Christ. And it encompasses that whole company of
Christians—past, present, and yet unborn—who are
called by God into fullness of life. In the biblical tradition it is important to remember that many of the metaphors used in Scripture to enrich our understanding of
the church presume the widest and most far-reaching
definition.

When we dig deeply into the biblical texts, we can
discover the ways in which Christians throughout church
history have come to name the community of believers.
The English word "church" comes from the Greek
adjective *kuriakos,* meaning "the Lord's" or "belonging
to the Lord." Other forms of this word are found in the
German *Kirche,* Swedish *kyrka,* Gaelic *kirk,* and Russian
tserkov.

A more important word, from the biblical standpoint, is
ekklesia. We derive the English adjective "ecclesiastical" from this Greek noun. *Ekklesia* is related to the verb
ekkaleo, meaning "to call out" or "to summon." In
classical Greece this was not a particularly religious
word. For several centuries before the time of Christ it
had been used among Greeks to describe an assembly of
the whole body of citizens who met together to elect
magistrates, to confirm political decisions, and to hear
appeals arising from judicial decisions. Any responsible
assembly called together by political authorities to do
business was considered an *ekklesia.*

Also, in the Greco-Roman world when the Jewish
Scriptures were translated into Greek, the word *ekklesia*
was used throughout that translation (known as the
Septuagint) in several ways. It was used in stories that
tell of a company summoned by a trumpet to learn the
word of God (Num. 10). It described assemblies held by
the Hebrews traveling in the wilderness under God's

leadership (Deut. 9; 10). Eventually it came to refer to the whole people of God, those whom God has called.

Ekklesia is also found in the Septuagint as the translation of the Hebrew word that means "synagogue," the particular meeting place of Jews for worship. Yet in some places this very same Hebrew word was translated "congregation." Therefore, as time went on, *ekklesia* came to refer to both: a total people called by God and a particular group meeting in one place.

When the early Christians began writing letters and sought to describe the uniqueness of their community, they naturally used *ekklesia*. They believed that they were a people called by God into a new era. For the early church this special sense of calling, and eventually the universality of the call, became an important emphasis. Because Hellenistic Jews who were scattered around the Mediterranean commonly called their worshiping center and assembly a synagogue, by using the word *ekklesia* the new Christians were able to distinguish themselves from the Jewish community. It may be that the continuing secular use of this word in Hellenistic society made the label especially appealing to Gentile Christians.

Jesus himself said almost nothing about the church. In fact, the word *ekklesia* occurs only twice in the four Gospels: first, in a passage where Jesus says that he will build his church on this rock (Matt. 16:18) and, second, in some words about discipline where he advises that the sin of an unrepentant disciple ought to be told to the church (Matt. 18:17). It is in the writings of the apostle Paul that a unique "ecclesiology," or doctrine of the church, takes shape.

Throughout the development of the Scriptures and church history the word *ekklesia* assumes new meaning and increasing power. It builds upon the understandings of special calling which pervade the Old Testament, and

it enriches and expands these meanings to define a new
people who live with Jesus Christ.

> This title makes it clear not only that, as with the Old
> Testament Church, it is not just a human assembly but is
> one formed by the act of God, but also that as distinguished
> from the Old Testament Church, it is formed through the
> work of Christ. Accordingly, when the New Testament
> speaks about the Church, it refers to the company of people
> who have been called to respond to the gracious invitation
> of God through Jesus Christ and have obeyed. They form a
> new "people of God" which does not depend on being of
> the same race or on anything which they themselves have
> chosen or achieved, but depends solely on salvation
> through Jesus Christ. (William Stewart, *The Nature and
> Calling of the Church,* p. 8)

IMAGES AND METAPHORS

To a person in today's world much of this theological
language and concern about the nature of the church may
seem labored. The conviction, however, that the church
we experience in popular culture, and the church we
appreciate quite personally, is ultimately created by
God—this conviction is fundamental to the biblical perspective. It is further complicated by the fact that biblical
language is rich with metaphors and images quite foreign
to twentieth-century scientific rationality. How do we
find any kinship with a wandering band of Galilean
disciples? How do we translate the radical pacifism and
isolation of those first Christians into ethical actions
appropriate to a church that is often aligned with political
power? How do we remember that the church began as a
radical lay organization, when it seems to be dominated
by a priestly hierarchy or professional clique? How do
we value the archaic mythology of heaven and hell,
when we know the earth is a sphere? These and many
other questions point out the difficulties of fully appreci-
ating biblical material.

Paul S. Minear's book *Images of the Church in the New Testament* has explored this problem carefully. He suggests that we could adopt the methods of study appropriate to the mind of the New Testament church (a way of thinking dominated by pictures, analogies, and images), but we might fail to communicate with a contemporary audience. On the other hand, we could proceed to use the most modern methods, but when we do that we are likely to miss the richness and spirit of the ancient texts. The solution is a careful recovery of the ways by which communal imagination shapes conceptual thinking in all times and places. If we can recognize that the images and metaphors in the Scriptures (especially concerning the church) draw upon the collective experience of a community and if we can help modern communities of faith explore some of the same experiences, we may be able to recover the use of biblical images. (Paul S. Minear, *Images of the Church in the New Testament*, pp. 16–17.)

Images are language pictures. They serve as tools of rhetoric which help us describe and convey an impression concerning something we already know. They provide the means to describe a reality that is not clearly visible or expressed by other kinds of language. And they sometimes provide a way to enhance self-understanding or enrich community knowledge.

> The eternal gulf between being and idea can only be bridged by the rainbow of imagination. The word-bound concept is always inadequate to the torrent of life. Hence it is only the image-making or figurative word that can invest things with expression and at the same time bathe them in the luminosity of ideas: idea and thing are united in the image. But whereas the language of ordinary life—in itself a working and workmanlike instrument—is continually wearing down the image content of words and acquiring a superficial existence of its own (logical only in appearance), poetry continues to cultivate the figurative, i.e.,

image-bearing qualities of language, with deliberate intent. (Johan Huizinga, *Homo Ludens*, p. 4)

Biblical and theological understandings of the church begin with images and metaphors. The ancient scriptures abound in word pictures that build upon a shared life of faith. In such words the imagination of the community is reflected and nourished. Therefore, to examine the church from the biblical and theological perspective we are led to consider three dominant images which Christians use to speak of the church.

THE CHURCH AS THE PEOPLE OF GOD

In Christian thinking, God is the author of life and is especially concerned with human happiness. In one sense it is possible to say that the church began with creation. God looked at all that was made and called it "good." God placed humanity in divine-human relationship and in human community. God expected human creatures to use the rhythm and harmony of nature for constructive ends. And God asked only that men and women acknowledge divine authority. This view of human nature emphasizes its obligations and its freedoms. It claims that God creates us with ability for friendship and loyalty; and that God calls us to respond.

The biblical record, however, explains that God's intention was not fulfilled. Women and men have refused over and over to live in loyalty and trust. They have rebelled against God and suffered the consequences. The Genesis stories of a garden, a murder, a flood, and a tower spell out the tale of human disaster. For not only do human creatures deny the rule of God, they cannot even live with each other.

Biblical faith insists that God does not give up. God was not content to have the creation plan destroyed by human sin. God decided to meet the problem of human rebellion by choosing one people to become a means of blessing for all the nations of the earth; a chosen people. Thus God took the initiative to call Abraham and Sarah to lives of faith, loyalty, and trust. "Go from your country and your kindred and your father's house to the land that I will show you. And I will make of you a great nation, and I will bless you, and make your name great, so that you will be a blessing. I will bless those who bless you, and [one] who curses you I will curse; and by you all the families of the earth shall bless themselves" (Gen. 12:1–3). In the early church when Christians spoke of their spiritual ancestors in the faith they remembered Abraham and Sarah who obeyed when they were called to go out, not even knowing where they were to go. They believed that all those who placed their trust in the promises of God were part of the church (Heb. 11:8–12).

Two things are important about this call: the promises are not for Abraham and Sarah alone and they are not exclusively for their descendants, for "by you all the families of the earth shall bless themselves." God purposed to use the faith of this family as a means to redeem all peoples. But God also reminded them that only as they kept faith would blessings, not curses, fall upon them. The tragedy of the story is that later descendants came to interpret God's choice as privilege rather than responsibility.

In Christian theology the call to Abraham and Sarah is the foundation for what comes to be known as the covenant. It has historical grounding in the promises of particular persons. It is initiated by God. It is not an agreement between equals. And it depends solely upon God's mercy. To be "elected," therefore, is the same as to be "loved." "It was not because you were more in number than any other people that the LORD set [divine] love upon you and chose you, for you were the fewest of all peoples; but it is because the LORD loves you, and is keeping the oath" (Deut. 7:7–8). Finally, the covenant demands response through action and worship. Although it begins with the special commitment of God to particular persons, it reflects the promises of God to all people.

In the history of Israel the covenant is renewed and formalized during the escape from Egypt and those years of wandering in the wilderness (the exodus). When the people are slaves in Egypt under foreign rule, God calls Moses to deliver them from bondage. God tells Moses, "I have seen the affliction of my people who are in Egypt, and have heard their cry because of their taskmasters; I know their sufferings, and I have come down to deliver them out of the hand of the Egyptians, and to bring them up out of that land to a good and broad land, a land flowing with milk and honey" (Ex. 3:7–8). During the many years in the wilderness following their deliverance the people learn what it means to be a "covenant people." Through Moses they hear God's commands. "I am the Lord your God, who brought you out of the land of Egypt, out of the house of bondage" (Ex. 20:2). Therefore, they are to have no other gods, make no graven images, not take the Lord's name in vain, keep the Sabbath, honor their parents, and not kill, commit adultery, steal, bear false witness, or covet a neighbor's possessions. These Ten Commandments, and many other laws, become the obligations of the covenant.

Later God gives Israel a king. For a time the nation prospers and the people enjoy the Promised Land. In time, however, they forsake the covenant. The fortunes of Israel wane and prophets call the people back to God. Hosea grieves over the disobedience of Israel, but trusts that God will not forget. The theme of a called and chosen people appears again and again. "When Israel was a child, I loved him, and out of Egypt I called my son. The more I called them, the more they went from me. . . . How can I give you up, O Ephraim! How can I hand you over, O Israel! . . . I will not execute my fierce anger, . . . for I am God and not [human], the Holy One in your midst, and I will not come to destroy" (Hos. 11:1–2, 8–9).

Still later the prophet Jeremiah challenged Israel to return to the Lord and promised that God would make a new covenant:

> Behold, the days are coming, says the LORD, when I will make a new covenant with the house of Israel and the house of Judah, not like the covenant which I made with their [ancestors] when I took them by the hand to bring them out of the land of Egypt, my covenant which they broke, though I was their husband, says the LORD. But this is the covenant which I will make with the house of Israel after those days, says the LORD: I will put my law within them, and I will write it upon their hearts; and I will be their God, and they shall be my people. (Jer. 31:31–33)

The spiritual leaders of Israel debated how God would make that people. Some anticipated a new leader, one anointed by God (Isa. 11). Others envisioned a "Son of man" who would become a "watchman for the house of Israel" (Ezek. 3). Still others hoped for a new pouring out of the Holy Spirit (Ezek. 37 and Joel 2), or a remnant that would repent (Isa. 10). Much later Christians looked upon the description of a suffering servant (Isa. 53) as significant. Eventually, the Christian church interpreted Jesus as the fulfillment of all these covenant promises.

The image of being a people is fundamental to any understanding of the church. As a people who are heirs of a covenant now fulfilled through the life, death, and resurrection of Jesus, the church defines itself as a people called by God. The earliest disciples celebrated their life in a new community. Although they had scattered and dispersed during Jesus' trial and death, at Pentecost they came "together in one place" and experi-

enced the renewing power of the living Christ. On
Pentecost (often called the birthday of the church) Peter
declared that the promises of the Scriptures were fulfilled through Jesus Christ. When the people asked what
they should do, Peter said: "Repent, and be baptized
every one of you in the name of Jesus Christ for the
forgiveness of your sins; and you shall receive the gift of
the Holy Spirit. For the promise is to you and to your
children and to all that are far off, every one whom the
Lord our God calls" (Acts 2:38–39). When the day was
over, those who responded were bound together into a
new people. "All who believed were together and had all
things in common; and they sold their possessions and
goods and distributed them to all as any had need. And
day by day, attending the temple together and breaking
bread in their homes, they partook of food with glad and
generous hearts, praising God and having favor with all
the people" (Acts 2:44–47). Later, Paul writes to the
Christians at Rome, quoting from Hosea and emphasizing that the church is now God's people: "Those who
were not my people, I will call 'my people,' and her who
was not beloved I will call 'my beloved.' And in the very
place where it was said to them, 'You are not my people,'
they will be called '[children] of the living God' " (Rom.
9:25–26).

The image of the church as the people of God is
fundamental. This people may have existed earlier, but
never fully. God in Christ defines or calls the church as a
chosen people. And the calling carries responsibilities.
"You are a chosen race, a royal priesthood, a holy nation,
God's own people, that you may declare the wonderful
deeds of [God] who called you out of darkness into
[God's] marvelous light. Once you were no people but
now you are God's people; once you had not received

mercy but now you have received mercy" (I Peter 2:9–10).

In the early church there was some argument over whether the new covenant in Jesus Christ was for everyone, or only for Israel. Paul insisted that all people of faith are spiritual descendants of Israel and "children of the promise" (Rom. 9:6–8). He affirmed that in the church there is neither Jew nor Greek, slave nor free, male nor female, for we are all one in Christ Jesus (Gal. 3:28).

In summary, to be the "people of God" is defined by God. It is never limited by human definitions. And it is a shared experience. In modern society, where the emphasis is often on the individual and one's personal freedom, this image of being a people is important. The church is not a conglomeration of independent believers who sense God's call. As Hans Küng writes: "The church begins, not with a pious individual, but with God. The pious individual cannot by himself [or herself] achieve the transformation of isolated sinful men [and women] into the people of God" (Hans Küng, *The Church*, p. 24). To call the church the "people of God" builds upon Old Testament images of nation, election, inheritance, and obligation. It also expresses corporate images of pastoral flocks and crowded cities. In all cases

> the galaxy of images that oscillate around this conception served in a distinctive way to place the New Testament church in the setting of the long story of God's dealings with [God's] chosen people. To apply this analogy to the Christian community was to assert an enduring solidarity with that Israel of whose story the Law and the Prophets provided the authoritative account. The early Christians did not date the beginnings of God's people from Jesus' birth or ministry, from his Eucharistic feast or resurrection, or even from the descent of the Spirit at Pentecost, but from

the covenant-making activity of God in the times of Abraham and Moses. (Minear, *Images of the Church in the New
Testament,* p. 70)

The Church as the Body of Christ

Another way to emphasize that the nature of the
church is much more than popular or personal opinion is
to speak of the church as the body of Christ. This is a very
important biblical image.

Jesus believed that God had great purpose in calling
Israel, and he considered himself sent by God for a task
that was unique. He called people to follow him and he
spoke with authority. His vision of his mission was
obviously wider than common Jewish expectations.
Therefore, the "new people" who followed Jesus believed that they enjoyed a special relationship to him.
Although the phrase "body of Christ" never appears in
the Gospels or the book of The Acts, Paul refers to the
church as the body of Christ many times. It is fundamental to the New Testament understanding of the church.
What does it mean?

Calling the church the body of Christ carries a powerful ambiguity. On the one hand, it refers to the group of
believers who follow Christ and embody his ongoing
presence on earth through the organizational church. On
the other hand, it clearly points to the death of Christ on
the cross and the conviction that sharing bread and wine
allows every believer in some way to be part of that
sacrificed body. The image is strengthened because the
lines between the body of believers and Christ's body
remain forever blurred.

Paul writes about the body of Christ in many places. It
is the church. It is a way of highlighting how the church
is more than any human club or organization. It is an
organic metaphor that describes the church in the world.
It becomes a model for internal patterns of authority; and

it affirms the mystery of Christ's ongoing presence with all Christians.

The body of Christ is much greater than one particular gathering of believers. It has cosmic and universal reality. It lives under the headship of Christ. It contains the fullness of God and triumphs over all human principalities and powers (Eph. 1:20–23). Christians, therefore, should not be misled by competing world views or loyalties. The body of Christ is literally the church in all times and places.

The most extensive use of this image in the New Testament explores the ways a particular church community ought to see and understand itself.

> For just as the body is one and has many members, and all the members of the body, though many, are one body, so it is with Christ. For by one Spirit we were all baptized into one body—Jews or Greeks, slaves or free—and all were made to drink of one Spirit.
>
> For the body does not consist of one member but of many. If the foot should say, "Because I am not a hand, I do not belong to the body," that would not make it any less a part of the body. . . . But as it is, God arranged the organs in the body, each one of them, as [God] chose. If all were a single organ, where would the body be? As it is, there are many parts, yet one body. . . . But God has so composed the body, giving the greater honor to the inferior part, that there may be no discord in the body, but that the members may have the same care for one another. . . .
>
> Now you are the body of Christ and individually members of it. And God has appointed in the church first apostles, second prophets, third teachers, then workers of miracles, then healers, helpers, administrators, speakers in various kinds of tongues. (I Cor. 12:12–15, 18–20, 24–25, 27–28)

The image of the body as explored by Paul provides helpful ways to speak about unity and growth, varieties of gifts, and patterns of authority. First, the church is organic. It is made up of many parts, but it is never viewed simply as a conglomeration. The sum is greater than all of the parts, just as a person is more than all of his or her limbs or senses. Furthermore, the growth and health of the church is grounded in love which matures in faith. To be part of the church is an evolving and organic experience, because the church is the body of Christ, not a secular institution.

Secondly, when Christians come together in Christ all of their gifts are important. If they are inspired by the same spirit and glorify or enrich the common good, they have equal value. This means that the church, as the body of Christ, needs every gift. We should not assume that what the clergy do or say is any more important than the gifts of the laity. "God arranged the organs in the body, each one of them"—all are needed for good health.

Thirdly, viewing the church as the body of Christ emphasizes strongly the authority of Christ as the head of the church. If Christians are "to grow up in every way into him who is the head, into Christ, from whom the whole body, joined and knit together by every joint with which it is supplied" (Eph. 4:15–16), they must remember that the body exists by the authority of the head. The earliest Christian creed contained four words: "Jesus Christ is Lord" (Phil. 2:11). In a world with many competing loyalties the testimony of Christians is that Jesus Christ makes a difference.

To be the church is to confess the faith that Jesus Christ makes possible a new covenant with God. The church is a New Israel embodying the ancient witness and a new mission. From the first century to the present, Christians have proclaimed the conviction that "in him all things hold together. He is the head of the body, the church; he is the beginning, the first-born from the dead, that in everything he might be pre-eminent. For in him all the fulness of God was pleased to dwell" (Col. 1:17–19). Whether or not there are other equally valuable witnesses for our times does not concern the Christian. Faith in Christ is all-sufficient.

Finally, the image of the body of Christ is filled with powerful reminders of the last supper of Jesus and the importance of being "in" or "with" Christ by sharing bread and wine. Christians remember that on the night when Jesus was betrayed he took bread, "and when he had given thanks, he broke it, and said, 'This is my body which is for you. Do this in remembrance of me.' In the same way also the cup, after supper, saying, 'This cup is the new covenant in my blood. Do this, as often as you drink it, in remembrance of me.' For as often as you eat this bread and drink the cup, you proclaim the Lord's death until he comes" (I Cor. 11:24–26). Christians have argued repeatedly about how Christ is present in the Sacrament, but all agree that this holy meal is extraordinary. To be nourished by the bread and the cup places every Christian in a unique relationship to Christ, as well as to the company of Christians who follow him. To say that the church is the body of Christ carries with it powerful imagery about its divine grounding, its timeless reality, its internal organization, its loyalty to Christ, and its sacramental mysteries.

THE CHURCH AS A COMMUNITY OF THE SPIRIT

The church depends upon God's call to a people; and it claims to be the embodiment of Jesus Christ. It is also a community of the living Spirit. Although the church builds upon the events of history, it draws its present vitality from the ongoing presence of the Holy Spirit. To belong to the church is to share in the gift of the Spirit and to live in community by that power. This view of the Church emphasizes the sustaining presence of the everlasting God. It also highlights the contrast between the law and the gospel. Finally, it understands the church as a community empowered for mission in the world.

In the days after Easter the early Christians were overwhelmed with the things they had seen. They asked what would happen next. They accepted the word of the risen Christ: "It is not for you to know times or seasons. ... But you shall receive power when the Holy Spirit has come upon you; and you shall be my witnesses in Jerusalem and in all Judea and Samaria and to the end of the earth" (Acts 1:7–8). They did not have to wait long. On the Day of Pentecost the Spirit came like the rush of a mighty wind. In celebration they quoted the prophet Joel: "And in the last days it shall be, God declares, that I will pour out my Spirit upon all flesh, and your sons and your daughters shall prophesy" (Acts 2:17). They believed that a new Spirit-filled community had been founded.

The church stands, therefore, through the gift of the Holy Spirit. It was created by the Spirit and must be continuously sustained and renewed by the Spirit. The early Christians believed that they were literally made children of God by the Spirit.

If the Spirit of [the One] who raised Jesus from the dead dwells in you, [the One] who raised Christ Jesus from the dead will give life to your mortal bodies also through [that] Spirit which dwells in you.

So then, brethren [and sisters], we are debtors, not to the flesh, to live according to the flesh—for if you live according to the flesh you will die, but if by the Spirit you put to death the deeds of the body you will live. For all who are led by the Spirit of God are [children] of God. (Rom. 8:11–14)

In the early church there was much disagreement about the authority of the Spirit. Gradually Christians agreed that special gifts had their place, but unless the work of the Spirit enriched the community those gifts were not to be trusted.

Life in a healthy church is alive and vibrant. When

people have experienced the power of the Holy Spirit at work in their lives, it is natural to share and celebrate that joy. Churches are communities of confidence. Because it is normal to want to share the beauty of something or the sweetness of victory, Christians come together to share the gifts of the spirit. Individual faith is nurtured and sustained in the context of community.

But life in the church is also dependent and vulnerable. Christians are called to test the "spirits to see whether they are of God" (I John 4:1). To be part of the Christian community involves judgments and discipline. It is appropriate for the community to put limits upon individual faith and practice. And although the church does not deny the ongoing work of the Holy Spirit, it insists that the fullness of our knowledge of God gained in Jesus Christ will never be surpassed, only enriched. We worship one God, manifest as Creator, Redeemer, and Sustainer (the doctrine of the Trinity). Life in the community of the Spirit (the church) exists in this conviction.

Another way of emphasizing the importance of the Spirit in the church is to contrast it with life under the law. Paul's letters to the early churches do this over and over. "For all who rely on works of the law are under a curse; . . . Christ redeemed us from the curse of the law, . . . that we might receive the promise of the Spirit through faith" (Gal. 3:10, 13–14). "For. the law of the Spirit of life in Christ Jesus has set me free from the law of sin and death. For God has done what the law, weakened by the flesh, could not do: . . . in order that the just requirement of the law might be fulfilled in us, who walk not according to the flesh but according to the Spirit" (Rom. 8:2–4). In all cases, the community of the Spirit recognizes the authority of the law, but by God's grace through faith it is able to live in the Spirit. The Spirit is that gift which frees the church to be itself.

Finally, the community of the Spirit exists to witness to the world. In the life of the saints sustained by faith through the Spirit and freed from the law by the Spirit, there is also an obligation to the world. The Spirit comes to equip all Christians for mission. It is not enough to feel the power of the Spirit in the quiet of one's closet or in the household of God; the church exists to share the faith.

When the apostles were brought before the authorities and charged not to preach and teach about Jesus, Peter and the others answered that they had to obey God. They declared that Jesus, the one the authorities had crucified, was "Leader and Savior." "We are witnesses to these things, and so is the Holy Spirit whom God has given to those who obey" (Acts 5:32). The message is clear. Those who know Jesus as Lord are called to obey (i.e., preach the gospel), and those who obey receive the Holy Spirit.

Obedience in the Spirit consists of true worship and outreach. Jesus said, "God is spirit, and those who worship [God] must worship in spirit and truth" (John 4:24). To belong to the church, therefore, means to share the gift of the Spirit. It means to share God's love. Paul writes, "Hope does not disappoint us, because God's love has been poured into our hearts through the Holy Spirit which has been given to us" (Rom. 5:5). And once Christians have received God's love they are enabled to love others. "Beloved, let us love one another; for love is of God, and [one] who loves is born of God and knows God. [One] who does not love does not know God; for God is love" (I John 4:7–8). The church is a community of the Spirit which spreads God's love in many ways.

Biblical and theological understandings of the church can never be fully captured. They expand upon certain traditions and express the experience and convictions of believers. They refuse to see the church merely in popular or personal categories. They emphasize repeatedly that the church belongs to God.

There are many other phrases and biblical images which we might have examined here, but the message is the same. The church understood as "the building or temple of God," "the bride of Christ," "God's army," or "the new creation" still declares that the church is first and foremost God's. By considering the church as "the people of God," "the body of Christ," and "a community of the Spirit" we have explored three of the basic images or metaphors in our language of faith. This way of discovering the church not only expresses a classical trinitarian pattern, it is fundamental to any Christian view of the church.

4
FROM HISTORICAL PERSPECTIVES

Christianity is a historical religion bound up with one Jesus Christ. I heard of him only through the Church and not otherwise. Hence I cannot be content with a purely private Christianity which would repudiate its origins. Attachment to the Church is the price I pay for this historical origin. (Karl Rahner, *Concern for the Church*, p. 9)

Time is especially important to the Christian. We celebrate the development of a salvation story. In the fullness of time God acts. Christianity looks back to beginnings and hopes for God's rule in the future. Christianity marks special times and keeps a holy rhythm. The division of our common calendar into an era before the time of Christ and those years designated anno Domini ("the year of our Lord") witnesses to the centrality of history for Christians. Indeed, without our history we could scarcely describe our faith.

Anyone who travels in Europe cannot help being impressed with the residue of Christian history. Cathedrals, monasteries, frescoes, sculpture, and paintings tell and retell Christian stories. Cities rise and fall, wars are won and lost, leaders inspire and persecute, all in the name of Jesus Christ. Tourists are forced to absorb church history to understand what they are visiting.

We have already seen that Christians must rediscover biblical metaphors in any examination of the church. Now we will argue that Christians must take history seriously in order to understand the very nature of the church. But it is hard to know where to begin.

A *Peanuts* cartoon strip highlights the problem. "Church history," says Linus, "must go back to the very beginning." In great seriousness he continues, "Our pastor was born in 1939."

Where does the history of the church begin? As we have already seen, various biblical images of the church offer several answers. It began with Adam and Eve, called by God to faithfulness. It was restored through the promise which God made with earth's creatures in Noah's ark. It was sealed by a covenant made with Abraham and Sarah and sustained in the history of Israel. In the New Testament it could be argued that the church began with the birth of Jesus, or with his baptism in the Jordan River, or when he called the disciples to follow him, or on Easter morning. Many organizations use dates surrounding the life and death of their leader to mark their origins. In the history of the church, however, the beginning is none of these. The church began at Pentecost.

Pentecost was a Jewish holiday regularly celebrated a certain number of days after Passover. In Christian history, however, the Pentecost that followed the crucifixion of Jesus took on special significance. On that day the disciples experienced the power of God in a very unusual way.

The second chapter of Acts records that those who had followed Jesus were meeting together in Jerusalem. Suddenly they "were all filled with the Holy Spirit" and began to speak about Jesus with great enthusiasm. Even those who did not know the common language understood the message. Peter proclaimed: "Let all the house of Israel therefore know assuredly that God has made him [Jesus] both Lord and Christ, this Jesus whom you crucified" (Acts 2:36). On that day Peter celebrated the power of the Holy Spirit, but he also placed Jesus in historical context. At Pentecost, therefore, those who embraced the message redirected their faith and their understanding of history. "And the Lord added to their number day by day those who were being saved" (Acts 2:47).

From this beginning the church as the institutional expression of a new "people of God," the ongoing "body of Christ," and the personally experienced "community of the Spirit" began a long history. Although Christian people in many times and places have sought to go back to the first century and recapture the essence of the "church," it is impossible to get rid of the centuries of ecclesiastical life which shape our experience of church today. Just as we must use biblical metaphors and images to enrich our understandings of the church, we must use the accumulation of ecclesiastical history to discover still more about the church.

Yet the value of history is difficult to assess. If we seek to take history seriously, we are immediately confronted with questions of faithfulness and distortion. This is because the story of the Christian church is both a success and a failure. Depending upon how we look at it, the church is impressive in its capacity to survive persecution, infiltration, and apathy, or it is an embarrassing story of human failure to respond to divine love.

The history of the world has been shaped significantly by the spread of Christianity. On the one hand, the faith and practice of the church promotes an optimistic world view. Some scholars believe that this optimism has provided a positive environment for the development of modern science and Western civilization. At the same time, the failures of the church are clearly evident. It has repeatedly been unable to get beyond a rather limited perspective. The institutional nature of the church sometimes seems very far from the radical nature of the gospel. If the church comes from Christ, in its most authentic form it does not need Scriptures, priests, or Sacraments. Rosemary Radford Ruether writes that the church (as we know it today) was not instituted by Christ, but by "history." "The Holy Spirit does not underwrite any finalized historical structures or dogmas, but rather breaks apart and brings to an end such history" (Rosemary Radford Ruether, *The Church Against Itself*, p. 61). History is important, but it is also limited by human sin.

If we accept this critique, the church seems far from Christian. Nevertheless, history remains an important means for understanding the contemporary church. By examining four developments in church history we will have a better understanding of its nature: the adaptability of the church to the changing political order, the ways in which the church continually supports human creativity, the capacity of the church to reform itself, and the drive of the church to witness to the world.

ADAPTING TO THE POLITICAL ORDER

In the beginning, those who followed the Christian way were very few in number. At first they considered themselves a special group within the Jewish people. Gradually, however, the early Christians came to believe that the gospel could not be limited to people of Hebrew descent. Through the missionary work of Paul and others the Christian message spread throughout the ancient Mediterranean world. It was never easy to be a Christian. Christians were different.

In some areas Christians lived together in close-knit communities of economic and spiritual support. In other places Christians sought solitude and developed rigorous disciplines to keep their faith. These early Christians believed that the end of history was close at hand. They looked with eager anticipation toward a new era under God's rule. When they organized their earthly life together, they did only what seemed necessary to take care of immediate needs. Time was limited.

As history continued, problems arose. Christians had to deal with conflicting loyalties. For the good of the state, Roman authorities expected everyone to worship the emperor. Christians, however, refused to give allegiance to anything or anyone except Jesus Christ. Consequently Christians were persecuted and driven into hiding. They argued constantly over who was acting or believing correctly. Some became martyrs rather than compromise their faith. Those who survived organized church life and worship to protect themselves and to preserve the essentials of the gospel.

Persecution was the burden of Christian commitment during the first three centuries of church history. Understandably, during this period Christians were very concerned about protecting essential teachings and writings. Some of the earliest controversies in the church arose over which documents should be placed in an approved canon of Scripture. Christians also sought to develop regular patterns in worship and community life. It was a time when very basic assumptions about leadership and liturgy developed. And of course, because it was literally a matter of life and death, Christians were especially concerned about orthodoxy and heresy.

Not until the fourth century was Christianity tolerated by political authorities. Yet, in spite of difficulties, the church thrived as a persecuted remnant. In fact, there is some reason to believe that times of persecution have been some of the most vital and significant periods in church history. When it is not easy, Christians have overcome difficulties and transformed the world.

In A.D. 313 the Roman emperor Constantine issued an edict that finally gave Christians religious freedom. Suddenly from being an alien and unacceptable religion, Christianity became official. The church adapted to the changing circumstances. It thrived. Before long the overseers of various Christian communities (the bishops) assumed significant political power. As the strength of the Roman Empire faded in the face of barbarian invasions, bishops in the most important cities consolidated their ecclesiastical authority and assumed necessary political leadership. Within a very short time Christianity was the prevailing religion. Eventually the bishop at Rome became the spiritual and temporal leader of Western Europe.

During this period the church spent considerable energy organizing its life and thought. Great church councils were held to resolve some of the most important doctrinal issues: What was the relationship between body and spirit? Was Jesus fully human—or truly divine? Who could decide these questions? Gradually the church developed an understanding that orthodoxy could be defined by ecclesiastical representatives gathered to deliberate issues under the guidance of the Holy Spirit.

Questions of order and authority were extremely important. Whereas the early church had worried very little about status and social customs, as the church gained power and prestige it became more conventional. Women, for example, lost some of the freedom and acceptance which they had enjoyed in the earliest Christian communities. The church "fathers" consolidated spiritual and temporal authority. Eventually, patriarchs, popes, and secular rulers shared responsibility in temporal and spiritual matters.

Over time, churches in different regions developed diverse practices and theologies. Eastern and western traditions drew apart and became quite distinct. By the eleventh century there were two great Christian communities: one centered in Rome and the other stretching northeast from Greece into Russia. In 1054 they formally split into the two churches which we know today as Roman Catholicism and Eastern Orthodoxy. Although at that time the argument centered on the worship of icons (images or representations of sacred Christian personages), the reasons for division were deeply embedded in theological and political differences which had been developing for centuries.

Zealous Christians were convinced that they could reshape the political order to serve the cause of Christ. In the late medieval period thousands of people took up the sign of the cross to recapture the "holy lands" from Islam. These crusades were used by political rulers to squelch any movements that tried to challenge their control.

In western Europe the church centered in Rome wielded incredible power. It governed people and kept the faith without rivals. Periods of renewal and vitality came and went, but as the centuries passed, the Roman Catholic Church grew increasingly corrupt. By the fourteenth and fifteenth centuries there were many movements for reform. Scholars recovered knowledge about Scripture and earlier practices. Mystics explored new ways to God which did not depend upon the resources of the church. Even uneducated peasants knew that something was wrong. By 1517, when a pious monk named Martin Luther nailed his concerns for reform on the door of a German church, the pressures for change were well under way.

During the sixteenth century the Western, or Roman, church was split into many groups. Reformers called for a return to early church practices. They became known as "Protestants," not because they were protesting against evils, but because they affirmed certain basic truths which they believed had been lost in church history. At the Diet of Speyer in 1529 the Lutherans drew up a *Protestatio* emphasizing their primary loyalty to the word of God contained in Holy Scriptures. The Latin word *protestari* means "to make a declaration." Protestants sought to reclaim and uphold the faith in new ways.

Although some Protestants rejected political responsibilities entirely, most Protestant Christians continued to believe that the church needed to cooperate with political authorities and share political power. Some Protestants fought bitterly to impose particular ideas and practices on the rest of Christianity. When people believe something strongly, it is hard for them to imagine things differently.

Gradually, however, the assumption that the church had to control the political order waned. By the eighteenth and nineteenth centuries many Christians who colonized and settled America embraced the idea that the church could be totally separate from the state. This principle is commonly supported in many modern nations today.

The contemporary divisions of the church did not all arise out of a variety of responses to political power. Some divisons were generated by theological and liturgical differences. The story of the church as a political power, however, is an impressive and oppressive scenario. Even though the church is unable to claim such power today, it is important for Christians to understand the various ways that the church has adapted to the political order in the past. Two thousand years of Christian habits are not overcome quickly.

Supportive of Human Creativity

Christianity is a religion that takes this world seriously. It proclaims an incarnational theology and rejoices that

God became flesh and lived among people as Jesus of Nazareth. Even though it celebrates the triumph of God in Christ over death, it does not reject the values of this earthly life.

In the history of the church this theology has meant that Christians use creation to praise and worship God. And because some of the mysteries of the faith cannot be captured in language, the church has drawn upon the arts to express and preserve its work.

As the civilization of ancient Greece and Rome faded, the Christian church became a cultural as well as political power. The church shaped values and celebrated salvation. People gathered regularly for worship. Church leaders used many ways to help people understand Christian theology and practice. Plays based upon stories from the Bible were performed regularly in medieval churches. Bells, chimes, and special music called people to gather. Mosaics, frescoes, stained glass, sculpture, and architecture combined to bring only the best and most worthy aspects of human creativity to God. Indeed, the entire church building became a symbolic statement of Christian history and doctrine.

Once churches were allowed to function openly in society, Christians adapted existing secular structures for religious worship. The earliest church buildings were Roman basilicas, or courts of law. These large meeting spaces accommodated Christian worship and provided places for processions and sacramental life. Often they were decorated with mosaics or frescoes telling and retelling early Christian history. Most of the earliest basilicas used wood for the roof. It remained difficult, however, to make any very large roof of stone. After a time, builders developed a rib system which created a framework for vaulting larger spaces. The entire structure was supported on massive columns with quite small windows. From these principles churches could be built in the shape of a cross with a large dome in the center. Eventually Christians throughout Europe built great Romanesque cathedrals.

However, builders soon learned that the same benefits could be achieved by shifting the weight of the roof to large stone braces or buttresses on the outside of the building. It became possible to make cathedral windows large and colorful. Gothic buildings of great size and grace were built. What was important about the Gothic cathedral, however, was not simply its amazing engineering of space, but the way in which it integrated and expressed the faith through many art forms. In an era before printed books Christian cathedrals told the history of Christianity to people who could not read or write. Entire communities worked together to build cathedrals: hauling stones, carving doors and windows, and inviting the finest architects and artists to dedicate their best work to God's glory. Many cathedrals took centuries to build. Nothing was spared to praise God.

Church structures have always had an important place in Christian history. After the Gothic cathedral, Renaissance enthusiasm about ancient Greece caused churches to be built following the designs of Greek temples. Christians insisted that the church should use those arts most valued by society. Great organ and choral works were commissioned to enrich Christian worship.

In American church history people were very pragmatic. Early colonists borrowed from past artistic styles and created structures that combined practical and aesthetic needs. Although church buildings did not need to be "storybooks" of the faith, as in the days before the printing press, Christians knew that religious truths could not be captured simply in words. The church embraced art and architecture to express the richness and subtlety of the gospel.

Puritan church architecture was plain and unembellished. Not even a cross was visible, because Puritans did not want anything to distract the worshiper from the word of God in Scripture and sermon. On the frontier there were practical reasons for simplicity. Certain building materials were scarce. Furthermore, as the church became a center for education and community activities, it adapted. Black Christians developed spirituals and gospel tunes to express their faith. Over time the variety of ethnic immigration and theological traditions has produced American church music, art, and architecture of all styles.

Today the church remains true to its creative tradition when it combines music, dance, and the visual arts with spoken and written words. Christianity refuses to discount any aspects of human creativity. Our world has been greatly enriched through its support of the arts.

Church history, therefore, is never flat. It exists in the artifacts and monuments, the treasures and masterpieces, the concerts and drama of human artistic expression. It is the accumulation of centuries of creative artistic energy. Wherever it spread, the Christian church supported human creativity and offered the best of the arts to the glory of God.

Obviously, a different artistic story could be told by following the historical development of Eastern orthodoxy. In recent centuries the church has cultivated the arts of Christian communities in Asia and Africa. In every instance, the church celebrates the arts because it is only through art that the fullness of the incarnation can be shared.

Self-Reforming

One of the most reassuring things about this story is that the church also had the inner resources to purge itself of corruption and emerge with integrity. Over the years, concerned Christians began to ask important questions. Finally, in the sixteenth century Protestant Reformers began openly to challenge the authority and power of the Roman Church. Many movements arose which tried to restore practices and theologies that had been forgotten or distorted in Christian history.

Some people emphasized the need to retrieve biblical practices—for example, believer's baptism or more frequent Communion. Others argued for access to the Bible: Scriptures should be available to all people in their native language; bread and wine should be shared in worship; teaching and preaching should inform and inspire. Theologians debated about the Sacraments, understandings of sin and salvation, and the political responsibilities of Christians.

Eventually these and many other factors reshaped Western Christianity into a multiplicity of Protestant groups. Catholicism itself instituted reforms and underwent significant changes. The reforming zeal of earnest Christians was able to purge the church of many distortions and errors.

By the end of the sixteenth century European Christianity could be divided into five major groups: those who remained loyal to the pope in Rome (found mostly in southern and central Europe); those who followed the lead of Henry VIII, king of England, breaking away from papal authority but remaining theologically Anglo-Catholic (centered in England); those who drew inspiration from the theology and work of Martin Luther (expanding throughout the German states and into Scandinavia); those who built upon the Reformed traditions of Switzerland and the Palatinate (drawing upon the work of Ulrich Zwingli and John Calvin and spreading into the Low Countries and Scotland); and finally, those who rejected certain theologies (such as predestination), practices (such as infant baptism), or political responsibilities (such as military service). Historically, these people have been called the "left-wing," "radical," or "Anabaptist" reformers. Most of modern Christian history can be traced back to one of these five groups.

The arguments among Christians were bitter. Wars and political fortunes shifted and melted because of religious positions. Within each group, movements for further reforms struggled against conservative forces. As time went on, evangelical and pietistic revivalism accentuated differences. And because all of this took place during a period of extensive European colonial expansion, the divisions and subdivisions of Western Christianity spread around the world.

American religious life is a reflection of this situation. At the beginning of our history English dominance meant that Anglo-Saxon religious traditions prevailed. As slavery, immigration, and migration brought many Africans, southern and eastern Europeans, Asian and Hispanic peoples to our land, church history became more complex. Today denominational pluralism divides Christians into Roman Catholics, Orthodox, Lutherans, Baptists, Presbyterians, Episcopalians, Congregationalists, Methodists, Moravians, Mennonites, and Pentecostals (to name only a few). A recent reference volume on the religious bodies of the United States and Canada lists forty-six types of Baptists and twenty-three different Methodist denominations (Arthur Carl Piepkorn, *Profiles in Belief*). Other developments on the American scene have created additional diversity: Quakers, Mormons, Adventists, Christian Churches (Disciples of Christ), Christian Scientists, and Jehovah's Witnesses. Today Christian groups and practices are legion.

The global picture is even more complicated, because in the eighteenth and nineteenth centuries Christians from nearly all of these groups participated in missionary efforts to carry the faith around the world. Men and women of great zeal believed that the church of Jesus Christ should not rest until every human being had heard the gospel. They went forth not just to preach, but to overcome ignorance and disease and to care for others in the name of Jesus. In good faith they traveled to Asia, to the ancient Near East, to Africa, and to the native peoples of the western hemisphere. The church grew with incredible speed.

In most cases Christianity spread along with European and American civilization. Although many missionary societies and organizations tried to be ecumenical, new churches generally perpetuated past ecclesiastical divisions. Furthermore, the faith became entangled in Western cultural traditions. With the best of intentions Christian missionaries imposed Western values upon new converts and denied the worth of indigenous traditions.

This history of our church can be viewed negatively and positively. It is a story of reform and renewal alongside fragmentation and religious imperialism. We have worked for change and overcome corruption. We have been divided over differences; and we have been stubborn, even fanatical, in our insistence that certain principles should never be compromised. Our preoccupation with differences, however, has not been all bad. At its best it has encouraged people to hold to principles and to wonder at the diversity of God's ways. Through reformation and separation the church has matured and expanded its understanding of the gospel. In competition with other Christians and despite ignorance of non-Western ideas, the church still has made a strong statement about God and the world. If we become embarrassed and a bit guilty over the arrogance of this history, let us not forget that we have this treasure in the earthen vessels of history and that God both judges and forgives.

WITNESSING TO THE WORLD

Finally, we can view the history of the church in the world, rather than internally. In the two thousand years of its history, the Christian church has made an impact. It has sought to change the social and political order. It has cast judgments upon kings and queens, called armies into accountability, and raised questions about social justice. The church has served its own, but it has also served the world.

There are many ways that this story might be told, but let us highlight three expressions of this witness. First, there is the way in which the church continually challenges human understandings of authority. Jesus was known to begin many of his teachings with the saying, "You have heard it said, but I say to you." The church stands in this tradition.

Over and over Christian church people have looked at the world and questioned its assumptions. Human laws, political systems, economic theories, have all been subject to the judgment of the church. Christians have insisted that the ultimate authority is God, not human reason or logic. When nations set up laws to protect the liberty and freedom of citizens, the church remembers the frailty of human nature. When slavery refuses to honor the humanity of black people, the church calls Christian leaders into accountability. When women's gifts remain hidden behind social custom and rigid doctrine, the church offers the promise that we are all one in Christ Jesus. When war contradicts the message of peace so desired by the world's peoples, the church acts to break down pride and mediate between enemies. When colonial leaders ignore the perspectives of native and indigenous peoples, the church insists that God transcends cultural differences. When fear and shame confuse human understandings of sexuality, the church affirms our bodies as temples of God.

Christians stand in a world churning with competing values and possibilities and insist that all is not relative. Through the life and death and resurrection of Jesus Christ, God calls all humanity to a new way of living. It is not an easier way, but it is an authentic and saving way. It offers a peace which passes understanding, in spite of being radical and demanding. The church proclaims that Jesus Christ came so all might have life and have it more abundantly.

Secondly, throughout much of Christian history the church has not only stood apart from the world and declared the power of God's redemptive acts in Christ; the church has also invited the world to change. Often words were all that were necessary. Individuals, following Christian conscience, witness to the power of God in their lives and share that salvation with others. But the power of the gospel has not only depended upon converted individuals. Increasingly the church has recognized its collective ecclesiastical responsibility.

In our modern world where every individual is part of a web of interconnected social, political, and economic obligations, Christians have learned to witness through the collective ecclesiastical structures of the church. The church is called to speak and to act. It passes pronouncements and resolutions, it withholds financial support, it actively protests certain policies. Although Christians in good conscience will differ as to when such action is appropriate and how it ought to be taken, most Christians agree that our witness is communal as well as individual. The institutional church is called to actively engage the world.

And thirdly, the witness of the church is more than any personal questioning of past and present authorities and it is more than taking action in the complicated world of today. The church is a witnessing community pointing toward God's future and inviting others to come along. When Christians gather in churches to worship they believe it makes a difference. In the most trying and dangerous circumstances, under religious and political oppression, Christians worship. This witness gives others courage and hope even when everything seems lost.

Some writers have defined the church as both a means and an end. It anticipates a better time and it embodies that vision in the present. Spreading the gospel can be verbal and active. It is always important to share what we believe. However, the witness of the church is sometimes underground and silent. Yet, what the church is unto itself models for the entire world what God holds in store for everyone. We must remember that one of the most significant statements made about the early church had to do with the way Christians treated one another. People wondered at how those "Christians loved one another." In so doing the early church made a witness that pointed beyond the present toward a new heaven and a new earth.

The story of the Christian church has been told and retold many times. On the American scene patriotic pride has tended to distort our understandings of the church. We have claimed to be a "beacon on a hill and an exemplar for the world." We have celebrated the melting pot and gone forth to make the world like us. Sydney Ahlstrom notes that at the end of the nineteenth century "a new synthesis of American church history emerged— proud, nationalistic, and stridently Protestant." It was a powerful image, but it could not last. "Today the mythic quality of the American saga has evaporated." A new "post-Protestant" present requires a new past. Indeed, says Ahlstrom, "events have so radically transformed the American situation that our whole view of what is relevant in the past must be revised." (Sydney E. Ahlstrom, *A Religious History of the American People*, pp. 35, 29, 40.)

The Christian church is organic, and its history is dynamic. It grows and changes with God's people. At one time it may have been possible to see American religious history as a New World extension of Christendom, carrying on the legacy of Europe. But the stories of persecution, political power, human creativity, reforming zeal, and evangelical witness which we have highlighted above must be recast for our times. Discovering the history of the church, therefore, can never be finished; it is a process. In the effort, however, we are not alone. God has been our help in ages past, and is still our hope for years to come.

5
IN INSTITUTIONAL FORMS

There is continuity between the Christian community and other human communities. Common-sense observation makes this indisputable: people gather in appropriate buildings; churches have social hierarchies and political arrangements for the conduct of their affairs; an identifiable historical continuity exists through many generations and centuries; Christians have a common object of loyalty that binds them together. In these respects and others, similarities exist between the Christian community and the state, the nation, voluntary associations for charitable purposes, and many other groups and movements. (James M. Gustafson, *Treasure in Earthen Vessels*, p. 5)

We can discover the church in the Bible. We can discover the church in history. And we can discover the church in an evening meeting or an ecumenical council. We believe that in many respects the Christian church is a gift from God. It has been able to survive centuries of trials and change only through God's grace. Its history expresses God's plan for the world.

But despite such lofty claims made in good faith, the church is very human. It is an organization; a human institution subject to the same forces that shape and influence all human communities. It has a particular sociological character. It has developed certain patterns of authority and decision-making. It can be located in time and space. It shares a common language, meets natural needs for social fellowship, and cultivates specific loyalties. Out of shared commitments it sustains its organizational life and interacts with the world.

In church circles we are sometimes uneasy with the institutional church. It fails to live up to our expectations. Some people insist that they can be good "Christians" and never set foot in a church or associate with organized church life. In the mood of anti-institutionalism which pervades our society, Richard Neuhaus notes that "we too facilely posit form against reality, the institutional against the authentic." But, he argues, "institution is simply another word for social endurance. Even the most spontaneous and prophetic of movements cannot last unless they find institutional form." (Richard Neuhaus, *Freedom for Ministry*, p. 8.)

Neuhaus is right when he writes:

> I admit that I have never understood what people mean when they talk about "the institutional church." There is no other church of historical or social significance. It might be suggested that there is another church of theological significance. But the church we speak of theologically is not another church; it is this church—in all its sweaty, smelly, concreteness—although viewed in a different and more comprehensive perspective.
>
> The "true" Church of Jesus Christ is not to be posited against, is not an alternative to, this Church of empirical experience. The true church is the Church truly seen; it is this church transformed in the perspective of hope, based upon divine promise. (Neuhaus, *Freedom for Ministry*, p. 9)

In theological language we could say that the church is "incarnate." It exists in the concrete circumstances which affect every human institution, in the carnal, the flesh and blood of daily life. Sometimes it is hard to distinguish the Christian church from other organiza-

tions and that is the wonder of the incarnation. We
believe that God cares so much for the world that God
uses the human as a means for disclosure and action. God
literally invades history in a Bethlehem manger, in a
crucified prophet, in an ecclesiastical dictum. Therefore,
another way to explore the meaning and importance of
the church is to examine its organizational expression.

What are the various shapes and forms of the church?
Why are there so many different names and practices?
When will Christians stop arguing among themselves
and get on with their common calling? Is the diversity
and variety of the Christian church an embarrassment or
a blessing? These questions have plagued the churches
for two thousand years.

If we open the telephone book in any major metropoli-
tan area and look under "churches," we find that the list
is very revealing. More than anything else, the names of
our churches do not reflect our theologies as much as the
organizational and historical unfolding of our life as
Christians. Consider this list as typical: the First Community Unitarian Church, the Chinese Reformed Presbyterian Church, the Two Seed in the Spirit Southern
Baptist Church, the Armenian Orthodox Church, the Fire
Baptized Holiness Church of God, the African Methodist
Episcopal Zion Church, St. Mary's Polish Catholic
Church, the Seventh-day Adventist Church, and the
Lutheran Church—Missouri Synod. These are only a few
examples of the pluralism of contemporary church life.
Indeed, each one of these names tells a story about the
people that church serves, its theological traditions and
practices, and its organizational habits.

Why are there so many churches? Because people
experience the love of God in Christ in different ways
and in different places. Through historical and sociological analysis we can isolate four clusters of reasons that
explain the variety of the Christian church in our times.

THEOLOGICAL ARGUMENTS

It is hard to feel close to someone who disagrees with you about things you feel are important. We want our friends to agree with us. In matters of faith we actually need communities of support where we can worship and experience God's love together.

For this reason Christians have always argued over theological matters and separated from those who do not uphold the "truth" as they see it. Sometimes this has produced senseless division. At other times internal strife has stimulated needed reform and renewal. In the early years of the church an insistence upon uniformity protected the church from heresy and cultural accommodation. The church "kept the faith." By the fifteenth and sixteenth centuries, Reformers used theological arguments to call for a restoration of the biblical church. Although in the intervening years theological distinctions blur, most denominations still cling to special theological positions to justify their ongoing existence.

Theologically Christians have differed over the nature of God. Is God one? What does it mean to be trinitarian? Christians have argued over human freedom and the salvation process. Are we free to respond to divine grace, or is everything predestined? What is original sin? Should a Christian aspire to some higher level of sanctification or perfection through God's grace?

Christians have developed definitions of sainthood and celebrated Mary's virginity or mediating role. Many theological arguments center on the Bible. Is every word of the Bible directly inspired by God? Is it inerrant (without error)? In the divine economy what do we hope for at the end of time (eschatology), and what happens to human beings when they die?

Churches also hold various theologies of ministry. In

some traditions priests or clergy are literally defined as
the church. Where they serve and lead the liturgy, that is
the church. Theological arguments are made to prove
that ordained ministers must be celibate or masculine.
Definitions of lay ministry and religious orders draw
upon theological and biblical material. Even theological
education has been condemned when it fails to protect
the church from "the dangers of an unconverted ministry."

As an ordained woman in a mainline Protestant denomination, I know that theological arguments are very
powerful. As a church historian, however, I believe that
the Christian church has constantly recast the gospel to
meet its needs, and it will continue to do so. Our
questions lead to factions. Our answers are formalized
into denominations. Although differing groups sometimes accept the rights of others to their interpretations,
throughout most of Christian history those who deviate
from theological orthodoxy, as defined by others, are cast
out. Heretics are hunted and killed with Christian confidence. They need to be saved from their mistakes. More
importantly, however, the church has to be kept free
from error.

In more recent times Christian theological battles have
not been as dramatic. Yet, when we ask the question,
Why are there so many churches? we must recognize the
power of theological argument to enrich and destroy
Christian community.

POLITY DIFFERENCES

Although every church seeks to defend its organization
and structure theologically, many of the most important
differences between churches grow out of polity, not
theology. The word "polity" comes from the Greek word
polis, meaning "city" or "community." Words like "po-

litical" and "policy" come from the same root. Polity is the form of government of a nation, state, church, or organization. Every community needs structure. Polity is the glue that keeps the institutional church together.

From the very beginning, when Christians came together in churches certain patterns of organization and leadership emerged. The disciples followed Jesus. The earliest converts listened to the advice and counsel of those disciples. And when the church organized its institutional life, questions of power and authority were solved in various ways.

The apostle Paul recognized the importance of polity. When several early churches had trouble regulating their common life, he encouraged them to take responsibility. "All things should be done decently and in order" (I Cor. 14:40). But it was not simple.

Christians feel very strongly about polity. There is the story about a Congregationalist who was encouraged to embrace the ecumenical vision of the proposed United Church of Christ. He considered the issue and declared with some vigor, "I've been a Congregationalist all of my life, and no one is going to make a Christian out of me now."

There are various opinions about how much help can be found in the New Testament to guide the church in its institutional life. In varying degrees every group looks to Scripture to justify the superiority of its organizational pattern.

Over time, three systems of church polity or governance have emerged: (1) Polity may define authority as located predominantly in the clergy. The church is run by priests or ministers who are responsible for its institutional health. (2) Polity may use egalitarian and democratic processes within each local congregation or parish. The church is run by the people who elect leaders and vote on important policies. Or (3), polity may rely upon representational patterns within a particular community, or in broader assemblies. The church is run by elders or officers who derive their power from a larger body. In church history these polities have been labeled episcopal, congregational, and presbyterian. Variations within the three types become more complex when they are combined with the powers of secular rulers or governments. And of course, how Christians define their link to the first-century church and the earliest disciples leads to further subdivisions.

Churches that follow episcopal polity draw upon the traditions of the church, as well as Scripture, to defend their case. They believe that some forms of government found in the New Testament were intended only for the earliest years of the church. As the church grew and matured, the *episcopi*, or bishops, took responsibility to keep the church true to the gospel. Jesus had given certain authority to the disciples, especially to Peter; therefore it is appropriate for the later church to invest special authority on those persons who are the direct spiritual descendants of the apostles. Most episcopal polity justifies its form by upholding the importance of apostolic succession, whereby the earliest Christian leaders conveyed authority to later generations through prayer and laying on of hands. And within the Roman Catholic tradition the bishop of Rome, or pope, is a special "keeper of the keys" promised in Scripture to the descendants of Peter.

Churches that follow Presbyterian and Congregational polity consider the various offices and duties of Christian leaders in the New Testament church to be normative: the elders, or presbyters, and the deacons. They argue that the church should seek to pattern its contemporary life after the early church. But they disagree over what this means for church government today.

Congregational polity says that authority in the church

belongs to the whole congregation. Clergy and other leaders exercise authority only insofar as the people delegate it to them. Whenever the gathered church comes together in Christ's name it is fully and completely the church. It does not need priests or popes. Even relationships with the wider church are not necessary, although in practice they are very helpful.

Presbyterian polity comes down somewhere in the middle. It takes the patterns of the New Testament church and recognizes that its leaders have something more than the resources and authority of the community. The elders and the deacons are set apart by the church for ruling and service because they have been blessed by God. When they act, they represent both the people and God's will. Furthermore, the church is more than a local gathered congregation. Church leaders come together in broader assemblies to test the spirits and engage in wider mission.

These three polities define the many patterns in church government. If a church is labeled Presbyterian or Congregational, obviously its history has been shaped by polity. But even those denominations which seem to emphasize only doctrinal concerns are not unaffected by polity. Whenever a church engages in merger conversations or ecumenical dialogue, questions of polity become crucial. At times it may seem trivial, but Christians have divided and subdivided over whether a congregation can call its own pastor, whether the pope is the infallible head of the church, whether the actions of a General Assembly are binding on a local church, whether bishops should be elected or appointed, and whether anyone has authority to spend money or purchase property. Polity is important.

In certain periods of church history polity has combined with political authority to justify divine right monarchs and theocratic states. In modern societies which separate church and state, and where the church exists as a voluntary society, polity does not seem to make as much difference as it once did. However, we dare not ignore polity. If we know something about a church's polity, we know a great deal about that church.

When we ask the question, Why are there so many churches? we must recognize that ecclesiastical structures are not accidental. Christians in all times and places have organized their churches around principles deeply rooted in the Bible and history.

CULTURAL TRADITIONS

The organizational diversity of church life is a product of theological arguments and polity differences. It is also the result of various cultural and historical circumstances or accidents. Many churches are divided from each other because of language and ethnic differences. Germans and Scandinavians draw upon a common Lutheran tradition, but organize into different denominations. Various Scotch, Dutch, Swiss, and French churches all claim to be "reformed." Eastern Orthodoxy exists in Greek, Serbian, Romanian, Bulgarian, and Russian forms. Furthermore, as missionaries traveled to Asia, Africa, and the Near East they carried their ethnic and national traditions with them. The Reformed churches in South Africa and Indonesia have strong ties to the Dutch. French Jesuits and Spanish Roman Catholics influenced the western hemisphere in quite different ways. Today new Asian immigrants are bringing Western traditions once carried to their homeland by missionaries back into the United States. We can almost predict that Korean Christians will be Presbyterian and Samoans will be Congregationalists.

Race is another factor in the denominational landscape. On the American scene certain churches split in the early nineteenth century over the issue of slavery. Some of them have never reunited. Special black denominations emerged to respond to the unique needs of freed slaves. In spite of pressures for integration and equity, many black Christians prefer to belong to predominantly black churches.

Historical circumstances have shaped various denominations. For example, each wave of German immigrants that came to America in the nineteenth century came from a different area of Germany. Some Germans responded to Wesleyan revivalism on the American frontier, becoming German Evangelicals and then part of the Evangelical and United Brethren and finally part of The United Methodist Church. Prussian Germans called themselves Evangelical and in America they joined with the German Reformed Church (organized by Palatinate Germans) to create the Evangelical and Reformed Church. That denomination finally became part of the United Church of Christ. Saxon Germans brought great zeal for preserving Lutheran orthodoxy. When they settled on the frontier they established the Lutheran Church—Missouri Synod. Still other Germans from Bavaria were staunchly Roman Catholic.

Economic factors influence the institutional shape of the church. Sociological studies point out that Episcopalian and Presbyterian churches are upper-class denominations. Pentecostal and Adventist churches, however, have more members lower down the socioeconomic scale. Also, economic patterns vary from one part of the country to another. Northerners who travel in the South often marvel at the size and affluence of Southern Baptist churches.

Finally, cultural values and assumptions are reflected in internal ecclesiastical debates. Churches split over racial and sexual issues. In recent years many churches have been challenged to recognize the changing role of women. Whereas many Roman Catholics from North America and Europe believe that their church should change its attitude about women and the priesthood, this viewpoint is not held by Roman Catholics in other parts of the world. Each church responds out of its particular experience and cultural values.

The point is that the church exists as a product of its times, its languages, and its cultural assumptions. Sometimes it seems captive to these forces. When we ask the question, Why are there so many churches? we must acknowledge the variety of human societies. Sometimes the church fails to protect itself from local biases. The message of the incarnation, however, is that God enters into particular human communities in order to save us from ourselves.

PRACTICAL ISSUES

Finally, churches divide and split over very practical issues. They argue about the acceptable behavior of their members. They reject alcoholic beverages, smoking, certain kinds of food, dress, hairstyles, makeup, or recreation. Others regulate family life and control or monopolize leisure time.

Within Christian worship many churches insist that certain practices are essential. Divisions arise because one church baptizes infants and one does not, because one sprinkles and one totally immerses, because one has an altar call and another has an organ. How the Sacrament of bread and wine is shared becomes reason for division. Some churches serve wine and others grape juice, some wafers and others bread, some have a common cup and others use individual cups, some come forward and others remain in the pews, some welcome everyone and others close (or fence) the Sacrament to all but baptized members, some allow laity or women to serve and others insist that only a male priest can officiate. The Christian Church (Disciples of Christ) holds a Communion service every week. Unlike many churches with regular sacramental worship, the Disciples' service is led by lay leaders, not clergy.

Many churches use a prayer book or missal and others believe that prayers should be spontaneous. Some services have long sermons and short prayers and others are filled with music and pageantry. Some services are very quiet and others actively encourage worshipers to shout "Amen." Certain denominations are known for distinctive practices. They may wash feet, hold a watch-night service on New Year's Eve, speak in tongues, or spend an entire service in silence. They may have separate religious orders which allow individuals to devote their lives to special service or discipline. The Fire Baptized Holiness Church of God expects that every member will be able to witness to his or her second baptism (in the Holy Spirit) by speaking in tongues.

Divisions also occur because of the ways in which Christians choose to relate their faith to the world. Some churches are pacifist, refusing to participate in armed conflict. Others withdraw from the political order entirely and will not vote. Still others object to modern conveniences and avoid driving automobiles or using electricity. Many Mennonite and Amish churches fall into this last category.

Most Christians, however, believe that their church ought to engage the world. For some denominations this takes the form of missionary programs, for others it focuses on social and political issues. Many churches get deeply involved in local economic problems. Today, in some areas of the world, to be a Christian is a very radical and even dangerous position.

When we ask the question, Why are there so many churches? we need to recognize that individual practices and preferences divide Christians. It is a complicated picture.

BEYOND DIVISIONS

Once we become aware of the many theological, political, cultural, and practical reasons for division in the Christian church, it is easy to become discouraged. When will Christians stop arguing about the church and its institutional forms? Why must we perpetuate some of these old arguments and insignificant differences? There is so much that needs to be done in the world, why can't Christians get beyond the organization and concentrate on the work of the gospel?

These are good questions. There are two important ways in which church people today are overcoming the divisions of the Christian church. One is attitudinal and the other is organizational.

In the last four hundred years the Christian church has undergone great fragmentation and experienced amazing growth. Logically we might wonder how these two developments could have taken place at the same time. One reason is that people learned to "think" differently about the institutional church.

Instead of considering the church as an overarching organization aligned with political leadership to serve the entire social order by upholding Christian faith and practice, or instead of defining the church as a sectarian movement preserving faith and practice by withdrawing from the establishment, the modern mentality rejects these understandings of "church" and "sect." In recent times Christians have learned to think of the institutional church as "denomination."

The denomination does not pretend to have all truth. It is only part of God's church. However, this modest assertion does not cause it to consider differences unim-

portant. Denominationalism allows Christians to live in a
pluralistic world and accept the finitude of all church
forms without having to judge every other church as
totally wrong. Denominationalism frees modern church
people to appreciate Christian differences while preserving personal faith and practice. It generates a new
attitude about the church by recognizing that a certain
level of organizational diversity is a gift from God.

Attitudes about denominationalism differ radically. H.
Richard Niebuhr argues that denominationalism repre-
sents the moral failure of Christianity.

> It is a compromise, made far too lightly, between Christian-
> ity and the world. Yet it often regards itself as a Christian
> achievement and glorifies its martyrs as bearers of the
> Cross. It represents the accommodation of Christianity to
> the caste-system of human society. It carries over into the
> organization of the Christian principle of brotherhood the
> prides and prejudices, the privilege and prestige, as well as
> the humiliations and abasements, the injustices and in-
> equalities of that specious order of high and low wherein
> [people] find the satisfaction of their craving for vainglory.
> It draws the color line in the church of God; it fosters the
> misunderstandings, the self-exaltations, the hatreds of jin-
> goistic nationalism by continuing in the body of Christ the
> spurious differences of provincial loyalties; it seats the rich
> and poor apart at the table of the Lord, where the fortunate
> may enjoy the bounty they have provided while the others
> feed upon the crusts their poverty affords. (H. Richard
> Niebuhr, *The Social Sources of Denominationalism*, p. 6)

Others have not found denominations so deplorable.
Historian Winthrop Hudson argues that the denomination is not simply an accident of religious liberty or a
result of social class and caste. Underlying denominationalism is a new theory or theology of the church. It
was implicit in the theology of the Protestant Reformers
who insisted that the true church could never be encom-
passed by any institution. John Calvin wrote that the
whole question of the dimensions, the boundaries, the

limits of the church of Christ must be left to God. Therefore, according to Hudson, denominationalism becomes the basis for ecumenicity.

> No denomination claims to represent the whole church of Christ. No denomination claims that all other churches are false churches. No denomination claims that all members of society should be incorporated within its own membership. No denomination claims that the whole of society and the state should submit to its ecclesiastical regulations. Yet all denominations recognize their responsibility for the whole of society and they expect to cooperate in freedom and mutual respect with other denominations in discharging that responsibility. (Winthrop Hudson, "Denominationalism as a Basis for Ecumenicity," in Russell E. Richey, ed., *Denominationalism*, p. 22)

Until quite recently the Roman Catholic Church rejected denominationalism and insisted that the problem of Christian division could only be solved by every Christian recognizing the authority of the papacy. It considered other Christian communions, confessions, and groups, with the exception of the Orthodox, to be societies, not churches. Christian unity was available only through the Roman Catholic Church as the One Holy Catholic Church.

In 1959, Pope John XXIII began a process that changed these assumptions. He called for an Ecumenical Council which opened the windows for ecumenical dialogue and invited Catholics to view the church in new ways. The results of the Second Vatican Council, meeting from 1962 to 1964, continue to influence the life of all Christians inside and outside the Roman Catholic Church.

In the various documents of Vatican II the doctrine of the church is central. Christ established the church. The mystical body of Christ and the visible structures of the church are an "interlocking reality" found most clearly in the Catholic Church, "which is governed by the successor of Peter and by the bishops in union with that successor." Nevertheless, "many elements of sanctification and of truth can be found outside of her visible structure." The church is more than the hierarchy, for the whole people of God exercise priestly, prophetic, and kingly functions. And those churches which retain separate traditions outside of the Roman Church are linked together in many ways. They honor the Scriptures, believe in God and in Christ, are consecrated by baptism which unites them with Christ, and recognize and receive other Sacraments in their own churches and ecclesial communities. In a real way "they are joined with us in the Holy Spirit, for to them also He gives His gifts and graces, and is thereby operative among them with His sanctifying power." (*Dogmatic Constitution on the Church*, Chs. I and II.)

This type of thinking about diversity and pluralism in the church is very important. It frees Christians from defending dogmatic territory and leads toward ecumenical action. It acknowledges the need for unity, but avoids the arrogance of exclusivity. It has opened up a new ecumenical age for Roman Catholics.

Change has also come about organizationally. Within Protestantism ecumenical cooperation goes back into nineteenth-century missionary history. In distant and foreign lands Christians of varying persuasions needed one another. They worked together to translate Scripture and to meet human need. The old arguments and divisions of Europe and America seemed less and less important. By 1910 the World Missionary Conference brought together over a thousand delegates in Edinburgh, Scotland. They agreed that cooperation leading toward true ecumenical fellowship was needed. They continued to gather in great ecumenical International Missionary Conferences throughout the first half of the twentieth century.

On the home front, pressures for denominational merger and the reunification of fragmented organizational structures also grew. Lutherans from Germany and Scandinavia consolidated into several major denominations. Methodism, divided over the slave issue since the 1840s, reunited and eventually incorporated the Evangelical United Brethren Church to become The United Methodist Church. Congregationalism followed its ecumenical vision and entered into the United Church of Christ.

During this same period Christians responded to many new social problems generated by industrialization and modern economics. The Federal Council of the Churches of Christ in America joined with similar organizations in modern democracies to hold important ecumenical meetings in Stockholm (1925) and Oxford (1937). Whether or not Christians could agree on doctrinal matters, they explored common concerns for the life and work of the churches.

Still others insisted that Christians needed to examine fundamental matters of faith and order leading toward a common ground for unity in Christ. Evangelical conservatives challenged ecumenists to avoid theological relativism and syncretism. They warned against concentrating ecumenical energies exclusively on social and international problems, and neglecting the primary tasks of mission and evangelism. Faith and Order meetings were held at Lausanne (1927) and Edinburgh (1937). Although such gatherings did little more than list theological differences, the way was open for future discussion.

Finally, the ecumenical movement was greatly enhanced by the impatience and zeal of youth. The World Student Christian Federation, begun in 1895, kept pressing the churches to "overcome differences." And in the aftermath of World War II it all came together in the First Assembly of the World Council of Churches in Amsterdam in 1948. The Sixth Assembly of the World Council of

Churches met in Vancouver, Canada, in 1983.

International ecumenical organizations and efforts are always fragile. They depend upon the good faith and trust of individuals and the fortunes of war and peace. Until very recently they only involved major Protestant denominations and representatives from Eastern Orthodoxy. But that, too, is changing.

Since Vatican II the Roman Catholic Church has moved to stimulate ecumenical dialogue and activity. The Council, which included observers from many other Christian churches, stated that the sin of separation should be shared by all Christians. Those "who believe in Christ and have been properly baptized are brought into a certain, though imperfect, communion with the Catholic Church. . . . They therefore have a right to be honored by the title of Christian." Henceforth, Roman Catholics were encouraged to be in dialogue with these Christians. This dialogue leads to a greater appreciation of the teachings and religious life of each communion, to cooperation where conscience allows, to common prayer where this is permitted, to an examination of one's faithfulness to Christ, and to the undertaking of renewal and reform wherever necessary. "The holy task of reconciling all Christians in the unity of the one and only Church of Christ transcends human energies and abilities." Only through the prayer of Christ for the church, the love of God for humanity, and the power of the Holy Spirit will the unity of the church ever be gained. (*Decree on Ecumenism.*)

Attitudinal and organizational changes have allowed various groups of Christians to overcome differences and to cooperate in significant new ways. Union churches in Canada, India, Japan, and Australia set forth possibilities for organic merger. Federations allow Christians with common political and confessional loyalties to share their ministries. But the divisions caused by organizational and institutional differences remain significant.

There are good historical and institutional reasons for denominational pluralism in today's world. Our Christian names and practices reflect the varieties of God's people. And although we have come a great distance in our capacities to understand such diversity, we are far from "one." If the efforts of the Consultation on Church Union (COCU) are indicative, it appears that organizational convictions held by Christians around the understandings of Christian ministry and its authority remain extremely important to the churches.

> The theologies of all our churches all contain some distinctions between the doctrine of the Church and the Church of empirical reality. Some speak of the visible Church as distinct from the invisible Church, others of the corporal Church as distinct from the spiritual Church, others of the Church of ordinary history as distinct from the Church of salvation history, others of the Church of fact as distinct from the Church of faith. Some such distinction is obviously necessary. Apart from the promise, we could not surrender ourselves wholeheartedly to the ministry of the Church of empirical fact; to do so would be foolish; worse than that, to do so would be idolatry, giving ourselves to something less than the one who has ultimate claim upon us. (Neuhaus, *Freedom for Ministry*, p. 11)

The trouble, continues Neuhaus, is that we often permit distinctions to become separations. Thus we begin to speak as though there were two churches rather than one church. "It is easy to think that we love an abstract, spiritualized, de-historicized Church, just as it is easy to love abstract, spiritualized, de-historicized people. In truth, to love abstractions is not to love at all; it is but a sentimental attachment to our own whimsies" (Neuhaus, *Freedom for Ministry*, p. 12). The church of Jesus Christ may be incarnate, but it is also incarcerated in institutional forms.

6
AS DISTURBING PROMISE

Thank God, the gospel has interfered with my life in countless ways. When I have sought security, the gospel has pointed to loving risk for others. When my vested interests have blinded me, the gospel has beckoned me to open my eyes to the world beyond my own interests. When I get hooked on status and prestige, the gospel holds before me the picture of a crucified Savior. When I begin to think that my personal attitudes and acts are all that count, the gospel reminds me of my participation in powers and principalities, in systems and structures that by their very existence contribute to my advantage and to the dehumanizing disadvantage of others. . . . The autobiography of any Christian must surely be incomplete apart from the disturbing probings and promptings of the Christian gospel at the core of our lives. (William K. McElvaney, *Good News Is Bad News Is Good News . . .*, p. 39)

We can find the church in popular culture, in personal experience, in biblical and theological traditions, in church history, and in institutional forms; but unless the church disturbs us and invites us into God's future, we have failed to discover the most important dimension of the church. As one member put it, "The church is the only community or organization to which I belong precisely in order to be disturbed." This posture expects inquiry, inconvenience, and interference. It presumes that the human spirit will falter without God's love and care and that the church offers hope which goes beyond comfort. Being part of the church is a gift and a task.

Our Legacy

We have seen how the church is viewed in popular culture. It upholds human values and gives people a place to belong. It serves as an effective organization in our complex society. For some people it provides spiritual insurance against unknown futures and fears. The church is very personal. It celebrates and supports people from birth to death and throughout the human life cycle. When there are crises and troubles, the church offers help and solace. Of course, the church also serves the needs of special groups and responds to special interests. When it does this well, it grows. The church is a very human institution, which is appreciated for human reasons.

The church, however, is more than human. It draws upon a rich biblical and theological tradition. Through the metaphors and images of the past we experience the divine power and promises that inform and sustain the church. The church is the "people of God," "the body of Christ," and the "community of the Spirit." The church is a human institution, but the church belongs to God.

Furthermore, the church has a history and its history is part of its nature. Over time the church has shown an amazing capacity to respond to changing human circumstances. It has adapted to the political order. It has cultivated human creativity, especially through architecture and the arts. Although it is divided, it has moved around the world to witness that God cares for all human creatures. Today the church is known through its history in many times and places.

And finally, the church is an institution. For theologi

cal, ecclesiastical, cultural, and practical reasons the church takes various institutional forms. Sometimes there are profound reasons for division, and sometimes they are the result of mundane circumstances and human stubbornness. In more recent times long-standing attitudes about Christian differences and historic divisions have begun to heal. Through the ecumenical movement and improved Protestant and Roman Catholic relationships Christians in many churches are moving beyond sectarianism.

OUR SITUATION

What is the task of the church in our times? How will the church of Jesus Christ flourish and develop in a world that is undergoing significant change? It is important to recognize the dynamic environment in which the contemporary church lives.

The place and role of the church, which once functioned to order and regulate many aspects of life on the farm, in city neighborhoods, and in hundreds of small towns, is less influential. This is not to say that Americans are less religious, although that may be the case; but simply that we can no longer equate religious faith as closely with church involvement.

Furthermore, today's churches are engaged in new tasks. The population of our nation is becoming older. With fewer children and more elderly people the church is rearranging its priorities. Many churches have built retirement centers. Older members outnumber younger members. As the church adjusts to more senior citizens and fewer youth, its ministry shifts from education and initiation to maintenance and crisis counseling. People join the church to find a stable caring community in a rootless and mobile environment.

Gray hairs dominate our church meetings, but children

fill our church buildings. Many churches sponsor child-
care centers and offer supportive services for younger
families. As women seek careers and/or have to work
outside the home to "make ends meet," the impact upon
the church is significant. Women need help when they
try to balance new roles as workers, wives, and mothers.
Single-parent families are everywhere. And with the
rising divorce rate men and women cannot lean on family
relationships as they did in the past.

Furthermore, all of these changes create a volunteer
crisis in the church. People do not have a great deal of
time to give to the church. Commuting and leisure
activities take up the hours our grandmothers once spent
serving church suppers or making things for the bazaar.
Many people do not think the church has anything to
offer them. As a consequence churches are finding it
difficult to attract willing workers.

In this situation churches naturally lean more heavily
upon paid professionals. It is a complicated picture.
Within the Roman Catholic Church fewer men and
women are choosing the religious life, and there is a
shortage of priests and nuns. At the same time many
Catholic women are challenging the church to accept
their calling to the ordained priesthood. While official
policy still insists that only celibate men can be priests,
many women are actively engaged in parish ministry.
They are going to seminaries and pressing the church to
rethink its theology of ministry.

Within Protestantism opportunities for women in ministry have increased dramatically, but the demand for
clergy has not. Denominations that never ordained wom-
en in the past have altered their policies in the last
twenty-five years. Women are attending seminaries in
record numbers. But in mainline Protestantism these
changes come during a period of general membership
decline and economic inflation. The number of full-time

positions available in the Protestant ministry is shrinking.

Sometimes churches think they can "economize" by hiring women. Furthermore, many women with families are interested in part-time work. In the past when women have moved into professions previously dominated by men, men have ceased to find that profession appealing. Secretarial work and teaching underwent such a change in the nineteenth century. For these reasons some observers argue that ministry may become a "women's profession."

Among the growing evangelical and conservative denominations and in many ethnic churches women still exercise less direct leadership. But with women's opportunities in our society expanding, attitudes in these churches are bound to change.

The global and international context of contemporary life also has ramifications for the church today. Christianity developed in a European environment. It came to the western hemisphere about three hundred years ago. From its Mediterranean and North Atlantic foundations it spread to Asia and Africa through the efforts of missionaries. Until quite recently Christians have unconsciously assumed that Western cultural values were essential to the gospel.

Now, however, Christian churches in non-Western areas are claiming that historical Christian theologies are inadequate. They are limited by culture-bound ideals and presume the superiority of Western economic systems. It is difficult for Christians living on South Pacific islands to appreciate a sacramental meal of bread and wine when they have never even seen wheat or grapes grow. On the other hand, to share the power of the gospel in terms of the life-giving coconut is theologically relevant. "Coconut theology" and "water buffalo theology" bring the Christian gospel to a world far removed from the cathedrals of Europe.

The present conditions of the world further challenge our "Christian" assumptions about power and liberation. Not only do Christians in Africa, Asia, and South America develop new theologies, their views and presence cannot be ignored in North American churches. Immigrants from Latin America and the Pacific basin raise questions of economic justice and Christian responsibility. Our theology is challenged. How does the church embrace this diversity and preserve its identity?

Within American society the prestige of the church is debatable. Many people never go to church, and they question the importance of organized religion. Governments maintain a neutral stance. The church is on the defensive and has to prove its worth in order to survive. Many things once done by churches are handled by political and social agencies. People do not seem to "need" the church as much as their grandparents.

Statements and actions of the churches also have a decreasing impact upon public opinion. Clergy and lay leaders pass resolutions and participate in protests to express their Christian convictions. They are barely noticed. Some church members believe that clergy should not be involved in public issues. Ministers and priests, they say, are employed to service the needs of the institutional church and its individual members. When clergy take a stand on some matter, they are condemned or, even worse, simply ignored.

This attitude does not make any sense to Christians in those developing nations where clergy play key roles in helping native peoples win political and religious freedoms. Issues of economic and military aid get all mixed up with the gospel.

Finally, the church has new concerns caused by the advance of modern technology. Industrialization creates urban populations so vast that the delivery of services and the maintenance of law and order are almost impossible. Raw materials are being used so fast that supplies for the future may be in jeopardy. At the same time the accumulation of wastes in our air and waters threatens the quality of life itself. Pressures for living space and needed resources increase with each generation, often bringing famine and exploitation. As the interrelationships between human civilization and the natural world become more complex, the church can no longer deal with human needs unrelated to the rest of creation.

We are charged to be faithful stewards of the earth's resources for future generations. What does that mean? Furthermore, as we learn more about our world and the human body, medical science gives us new choices and ethical dilemmas. When does life begin? How do we balance issues of the quality of life versus the right to life? What do we do with Nature's mistakes?

In the past the church and God have been used to fill in the gaps of human knowledge, to explain when there was no other explanation. Some cynics say that the church has no useful function in today's world. Science and technology have taken its place. We can live easily in a totally secular world.

What does this mean? As a religious person I do not want to be secular. Secularity, however, is not always simply the opposite of sacred. In fact, one of the important dimensions of Christian theology is its emphasis upon incarnation. God is not beyond this world, God is here. The God of all creation lives in the sacred and the profane.

People may think that, because certain obvious signs of religion (such as the church) are no longer visible in the ways they once were, Christianity is suffering. In fact, secularity may be a blessing.

Dietrich Bonhoeffer confronted this question back in

the 1940s. He believed that we were moving toward a "religionless" time in a world that had "come of age." And he wondered about the significance of the church in that religionless world. If Christ was no longer an object of religion, but truly the Lord of the world, Bonhoeffer asked, "What is the place of worship and prayer?" God is not "the beyond of our perceptive faculties." "God is the 'beyond' in the midst of our life. The Church stands not where human powers give out, on the borders, but in the center of the village." Furthermore, the church must escape from stagnation and "move out again into the open air of intellectual discussion with the world, and risk shocking people." (Dietrich Bonhoeffer, *Letters and Papers from Prison,* April 30 and August 3, 1944.)

The challenge to the contemporary church is to embrace secularity, following Bonhoeffer's interpretation. This is not easy. It raises questions about worship and institutional resources. However, it may be God's way of calling us to faithfulness. The incarnation invites us to accept fully the fact that God is with us, "Emmanuel."

In our situation these are some of the forces at work to disturb our faith and our churches. Population shifts, the changing role of women, professionalized clergy, global pressures, scientific advancements, and a "secular" mind-set will shape the church of tomorrow. The church may become irrelevant, passé, self-centered, and insensitive. As one observer puts it, "The church is deformed by its struggle to survive." Yet, the church also has the opportunity to witness to the gospel in new ways. "New occasions teach new duties."

GOD'S PROMISE

The story of the Bible is that God cares enough to disturb us; to upset our life at the core and to challenge our comforts and habits. God appears in the midst of human sufferings, raising radical questions. When the first man and woman ignored God's commandments in the Garden of Eden, God asked them, "Who told you that you were naked?" When Moses confronted God in a burning bush, he argued, "Who am I that I should go to Pharaoh?" When the prophets called Israel to be faithful they reminded the people that it was "Yahweh" they served.

> The biblical revelation of God is one in which God comes again and again as a disturbing factor in the human picture—sometimes·from burning bushes, sometimes from whirlwinds, and at other times from pillars of fire. The procession of prophets is often a story of interference and interruption of injustices perpetrated by the strong on the weak. The prophets in various ways and through diverse styles call Israel again and again to renewed faithfulness to the covenant with the God of justice. (McElvaney, *Good News Is Bad News Is Good News* . . ., p. 35)

Dorothee Soelle has noted that the world is filled with people who live out their lives in hollow and meaningless ways. They are undisturbed and they are dead. On the other hand, she asserts, "To believe in God means to take sides with life and to end our alliance with death." It means to be disturbed out of our deadly habits. Natural death is not the enemy, "rather, our greatest enemy is the kind of creeping death, that living, breathing lifelessness we see written on the faces of so many in our day." (Dorothee Soelle, *Death by Bread Alone*, pp. 10–12.) If the church does not call us out of this death, it is not the church.

When God despaired over the evil and sinfulness of human creatures, the biblical record says that God decided to blot out humanity and all creeping things and birds of the air, "for I am sorry that I have made them" (Gen. 6:7). But Noah found favor in the eyes of God. So Noah built an ark and, when the flood was over, God remembered Noah and placed a rainbow in the cloud as a sign.

God promised never again to destroy the earth. "When
the bow is in the clouds, I will look upon it and
remember the everlasting covenant between God and
every living creature of all flesh that is upon the earth"
(Gen. 9:16).

In this story we have assurance that the disturbances of
God exist in the context of a divine promise. We are the
people of God who expect disturbances. We are the body
of Christ, broken and rejected for the sake of the world.
We are the community of the spirit following rainbows.

The Scriptures point out again and again that those
who follow the gospel are disturbed and disturbing.
They challenge principalities and powers. They turn the
world's values upside down. They identify with the poor
and the outcasts. When the disciples of John the Baptist
came to Jesus and asked him if he was the Messiah, he
answered them, "Go and tell John what you have seen
and heard: the blind receive their sight, the lame walk,
lepers are cleansed, and the deaf hear, the dead are
raised up, the poor have good news preached to them"
(Luke 7:22).

The future of the church of Jesus Christ depends upon
our sensitivity. We all want to hear the good news. But
what is it? William McElvaney believes that the good
news is really bad news for the powerful and dominant.
What is good news for the oppressed will be bad news for
the system of the oppressor. Yet, "if the Good News that
is Bad News breaks through a hardness of heart and
occasions repentance, the Good News for the weak that
comes as Bad News for the strong then becomes Good
News for all" (McElvaney, *Good News Is Bad News Is
Good News* . . ., p. 35).

For most of our churches the good news is difficult. It
says that God cares about the world and that the world is
made up of suffering people. Jesus did not walk with
folks like you and me. He spent his entire ministry

among the outcasts and scum of society, "the oppressed."

Contemporary liberation theologians charge that the cause of human suffering is not accidental. Human sinfulness is to blame. Granted, a certain amount of suffering is nobody's fault. Natural and environmental disasters cannot be controlled. But historical analysis shows that the patterns of life enjoyed by the powerful, the dominant, and the victorious have imposed suffering upon many. All political and economic systems oppress some people. And we who enjoy the benefits of those systems are, in some sense, the oppressors.

These are disturbing words. Church people, especially, have difficulty seeing themselves as oppressors. We go about our business with modest goals. We try not to waste food and we eat lower on the food chain. We recycle our cans and we drive smaller cars. We give to the church and work for good causes. It is not our fault that other people are oppressed. Most of us do not have enough power to oppress anyone, and we certainly do not have the power to stop those who do have power from acting oppressively.

Yet, the church as a disturbing promise also asks us to admit that we are part of the problem. We are unintentional oppressors through indifference and default. Our individualism allows us to think that if every individual embraced a new way of life, everything would be fine. But we are part of a system. Those of us who live in America, who consume a disproportionate amount of the world's resources, are part of economic and political systems that manipulate and dehumanize people. We cannot escape from the knowledge that systems which work for us often dehumanize and oppress others.

How we handle our knowledge about oppression is also important for the church. Rosemary Radford Ruether reminds us that it is difficult to maintain a "sense of just proportions" (Rosemary Radford Ruether, *Liberation*

Theology, p. 171). Everyone is oppressed in some way. Parents impose rules on children. Taxes limit freedoms. Crime is everywhere. If we are not careful, all of these things tend to dull our sensitivity to important distinctions between degrees of oppression. And when this happens we cease to recognize the desperate situations that surround the lives of many human beings. Our own problems may seem oppressive at times, but they cannot compare with the "oppression" of daily hunger and malnutrition, or indecent housing and rampant disease, or the tyranny of military dictatorships and the dangers of war. We need to remember that many of the world's people do not know where they will get their next meal. North American Christians should be disturbed by the injustices of our world.

Yet to discover the church as a disturbing promise calls us to realize the character of human systems and to exercise the influence we do have. We can vote. We can keep ourselves informed and take time to share opinions with others. Public opinion grows out of individual opinions. Although individual responsibility seems to be only a drop in the bucket, we have resources to make a difference.

Discovering the church means refusing to escape from God's disturbing promise. It means responding to that promise within a community of people who take the incarnation seriously.

OUR RESPONSE

One response to God's disturbing promise is to become paralyzed by it all. In our fast-moving world our capacity to know is sometimes overwhelming. Radio and television enter into our homes and bombard us with problems unknown to our ancestors. All of that information leaves us feeling helpless. So we protect ourselves.

We tune it out or we become numb. We avoid the pain and suffering of the world and become preoccupied with our private problems. Sometimes depression and suicide are the only alternatives.

The Christian church, however, is a community of hope. We are promised that God cares and that God will give us the power to respond. Discovering the church is not dependent upon us. God comes to us through the church. Even as we seek authentic discipleship, we are discovered by God. The apostle Paul affirms this when he writes, "For I am sure that neither death, nor life, nor angels, nor principalities, nor things present, nor things to come, nor powers, nor height, nor depth, nor anything else in all creation, will be able to separate us from the love of God in Christ Jesus our Lord" (Rom. 8:38–39). What response is called for from us?

First of all, Christians in these times need to come to grips with the decreasing power of the Christian church. Throughout most of church history we have enjoyed an establishment experience. We are a people with a majority mind-set. In the late twentieth century, however, the Christian church is not at the center of the world, it is on the edges.

As we have pointed out before, the pluralism and diversity of our global village is overwhelming. Although agnosticism and atheism have been around for centuries, the church has rarely existed in an environment so antagonistic toward religious organizations. Today, popular attitudes call the church to prove its worth. Many educated people question the value of any church. Christians must stop fooling themselves and admit that the church is marginal. Only then will we be able to make an effective case for its future.

The relationship of the church to the world's religions is also changing. Whereas in some arenas the church must confront antireligious humanism, in other places

Christianity is growing in direct competition with tribal religious and political ideologies. The church in North America and Europe has fewer members, but in Africa and South America it is growing with explosive force. Even if we say that the international church is not shrinking, the religious balance of the world is shifting. The Christian church remains the single largest religious group in the world, but it no longer has the prestige and power it once commanded. Nations with political and economic power ignore the church while developing nations (where it is growing) define the church in radically new ways.

On the American scene there are some important changes within Protestantism. Those churches which have been known as "mainline" are no longer as dominant or as influential as they once were. Since the 1950s they have actually lost membership. Today conservative and evangelical churches, independent congregations, and television evangelists have pushed mainline Protestants away from the centers of religious influence. Mainline Protestant denominations increasingly exist on the edges of power.

Although initially we may despair over this loss of influence of the church in our secular society, in relationship to the world's religions, or among Protestant denominations, our marginality could be a blessing. People on the edges of responsibility and power often have a special opportunity. If the disturbing promises of God call us to recognize the systems of oppression which destroy hope, we may be in a better position to offer the liberation of the gospel from the edges of power than from the center.

Secondly, Christians need to recognize the relationship of economics to the gospel. E. F. Schumacher insists that economics is the most important organizing principle of modern life. "Economics plays a central role in shaping the activities of the modern world." In fact, he argues, "there is no other set of criteria that exercises greater influence over the actions of individuals and groups as well as over those of governments." The church must become knowledgeable about economics, because "economic performance, economic growth, economic expansion, and so forth have become the abiding interest, if not the obsession, of all modern societies." (E. F. Schumacher, *Small Is Beautiful,* pp. 40–41.)

For too long the church has been insensitive to the ways in which economic systems support and distort the gospel. Yet the world desperately needs an economic design that upholds freedom as the responsibility to contribute to the common good rather than as a license to acquire material things. Those who call for new economic sensitivity in the church say these kinds of things.

A design supportive of people priorities will aim at the maximization of responsible environmental stewardship instead of maximization of profits; it will appreciate smallness and individuality while depreciating vast corporate systems which depersonalize; it will regard food and other necessities as a human right just as we now regard public education as a fundamental right; it will learn to appreciate growth in terms of human values rather than in terms of production or profits; it will think within a global perspective rather than a national one; it will increasingly understand the relationship between national security and people priorities; and it will explore the meaning of work and its relationship to other values, such as cultural, social, and esthetic. (McElvaney, *Good News Is Bad News Is Good News . . .,* pp. 76–77)

Christians in our churches will differ over many of these ideas. The point is, however, church members need to be faced with the interrelationship between their faith and economic issues. If the disturbing promises of God call us to deal with patterns of oppression and liberation, we cannot pretend that economics has nothing to do with our faith.

Once we have responded to the political and economic realities of the world, what are we to do? That is not enough and it will never be enough. At its core the Christian church is God's new creation. As members of that new creation, we have an obligation to worship; we experience God's love which enables us to love others; and we anticipate the promise of freedom in Christ.

From the very beginning of the church Christians came together to share the promise. Indeed, whatever else the Christian church has done throughout the centuries, the church has worshiped. Worship is not some extra activity added to build community. Worship is fundamental to the faith.

Scholars agree that the Greek term *leitourgia* means "service" or "work of the people." In ancient Greek cities every citizen was required to perform certain tasks for the public good. Later the Christian church used the word "liturgy" to describe the work and devotion of church people to God.

Regardless of its theology, history, or polity every church worships. And in certain common acts of parish life all Christians are bound together. We call upon the Holy Spirit to bless us through the waters of Baptism. We gather at our Savior's table to share bread and wine. We encourage our children to confirm their faith. We bless marriages and console each other in illness or at times of death. We set apart our leadership through prayer and the laying on of hands. We provide opportunities for confession, healing, and renewal.

Once a week Christians gather to keep the faith. They sing; they preach; they pray. Although the particulars of worship have varied dramatically over the centuries, worship remains at the heart of the church. Whenever Christians have allowed the discipline of worship to weaken, the church has suffered. If the disturbing promises of God call us to transform our churches into centers of hope where visions press toward God's future, then we must never ignore the importance of worship. Worship is the response of the church which draws from the past to enrich a future where we can be responsible.

In the church, more than in any other community, we know that we are loved by God and thereby empowered to love others. God calls us into the church long before we discover our need. God forgives our limitations and selfishness. God gives us strength to share that love with all the world.

And finally, within the bondage and obligations we accept in the church, there is amazing freedom. It does not matter if society is remade in a specifically Christian manner. It does not matter whether others agree or understand. In faithfulness to God "we are more than conquerors through [the One] who loved us" (Rom. 8:37).

Being part of the Christian church in our times is not easy. The challenges are great for the faithful few. God's disturbing promise calls us even when we are not worthy. When Dietrich Bonhoeffer examined the cost of discipleship he emphasized how important it was for Christians to engage the world to preserve the church. We do this, however, not simply to save the world. His words remind us that in the final analysis the world is where God claims us to be the church and we cannot find our rest in any other place.

> Let the Christian remain in the world, not because of the good gifts of creation, nor because of [their] responsibility for the course of the world, but for the sake of the Body of the incarnate Christ and for the sake of the Church. Let

[them] remain in the world to engage in frontal assault on it, and let [them] live the life of [their] secular calling in order to show [themselves] as strangers in this world all the more. But that is only possible if we are visible members of the Church. The antithesis between the world and the Church must be borne out in the world. That was the purpose of the incarnation. (Dietrich Bonhoeffer, *The Cost of Discipleship*, pp. 238–239)

QUESTIONS FOR DISCUSSION

Chapter 1. WITHIN POPULAR CULTURE

1. What are the reasons that you think people go to church?

2. What values do you think most people associate with the Christian church? To what extent do popular attitudes reflect realistic understandings of the church?

3. What influence, for good or ill, do you think churches have on our society today?

4. In what ways do you think churches should become involved in community and social change? How do you feel about people who relate to the church because of its position on social issues?

5. How does your church encourage community? How do you react to the charge that the effort to make people feel welcome sometimes distracts the church from its true reason for being?

6. Discuss the desirability of the church's having ways to screen members to prevent people from joining for the wrong reasons. What are the right reasons for joining the church?

7. How do you respond to people who say that joining the church is a "matter of taste"?

8. To what extent do you identify with the "grass-roots

mind"? How does it help the church? Are you optimistic or pessimistic about the future of the church? Why?

Chapter 2. THROUGH PERSONAL TESTIMONY

1. What are the reasons that you go to church?

2. Do you think that the influence of the church on society and history is waning? Why?

3. If religion is a personal matter, why should there be any problem with the church becoming privatized?

4. What are the most important points in your life history where the church was involved? Why are those times so important to you?

5. How has the church supported your faith development and spiritual life?

6. When has the church helped you deal with a particular crisis or problem? How? What gives people hope?

7. How much obligation do you feel to participate in the church because you want others to receive the same benefits you have experienced?

8. What is your particular attachment to a particular church? Is it the liturgy, the music, the preacher, the place, etc.? How valid or necessary are such specific reasons for belonging?

9. What do you believe are legitimate reasons for anyone to quit going to church or change churches?

10. Why do you think churches grow? Is numerical size important? Is homogeneity important? Why?

Chapter 3. WITHIN BIBLICAL AND THEOLOGICAL TRADITIONS

1. "When human beings open themselves to the 'new life' offered by faith through the Christ, they are the church." Discuss whether this means that the church exists without its clergy and without the Sacraments.

What makes a group of believing Christians a church?

2. Reflect upon the various ways the word *ekklesia* is used and understood in Scripture. How important to your "ecclesiology" is the conviction that God "called out" the church?

3. What images and metaphors in Scripture are especially valued in your understanding of the church? What images and metaphors hinder more than help?

4. How can the contemporary church recapture the biblical sense of being called by God to be a covenant people? Discuss the claim that such "chosenness" suggests an elitism that is unChristian.

5. Discuss the ways in which an understanding of the church as the "body of Christ" emphasizes its divine grounding, its timeless reality, its internal organization, its loyalty to Christ, and its sacramental mysteries.

6. In what ways do you experience your church as a "community of confidence" supported by God's Spirit? What are the signs of a church living in God's Spirit?

Chapter 4. FROM HISTORICAL PERSPECTIVES

1. What events in the history of the church are the most important to your faith? What disturbs you and what impresses you?

2. How have your travels influenced your understanding of the church?

3. How do you think the Christian faith has influenced the development of modern science and the course of Western civilization?

4. What aspects of church history do you believe are distortions of the basic Christian gospel?

5. Persecution has benefited and weakened the church in the past. What are some of the benefits and/or problems flowing from persecutions?

6. How should the church be protected and supported by governments?

7. What products of Christian creativity in art and architecture are the most important to your faith? How do you respond to those people who argue that these "works of art" are a waste of resources, because the money saved could be given to the poor or to others in need?

8. How important to you are the distinctions between the various denominations and divisions between churches?

9. Why do some Christians feel embarrassed over the historical involvement of the missionaries? What are the arguments for and against the need for missionaries today?

10. How can the church witness to the gospel of Jesus Christ in our times? What responsibility does the institutional church have for this world?

11. How does participation in the church today point toward a tomorrow where things will be different?

Chapter 5. IN INSTITUTIONAL FORMS

1. How does the institutional church fail in its capacity to live up to your expectations? What would happen if we got rid of some of the institutional structures and habits we find in all churches? What is essential?

2. What theological arguments or issues are important to you? How do you respond to someone who says these differences are irrelevant? What would you call heresy? How much variety of belief do you think your church should tolerate?

3. Is polity important to you? Why or why not? Which system? To what extent do you think that the Christian church ought to organize its life in ways that are different from the rest of the world? What principles in church polity do you believe are essential?

4. Most churches actually function with a mixture of polities: congregational, presbyterian, and episcopal. How does your church draw upon various polities?

5. How can the Christian church affirm the pluralism of our world and meet the unique needs of particular ethnic, racial, and cultural groups?

6. What practical issues surrounding life-style or ecclesiastical custom are important to you?

7. What do you believe are the biggest problems dividing Roman Catholics and Protestants?

8. Some people argue that there is more variety within denominations than between them. Charismatics, evangelicals, and social activists can be found in all denominations. Debate the claim that denominational commitments are no longer useful.

9. Discuss the impact of the ecumenical movement and the Second Vatican Council on contemporary church life. How important is it to continue ecumenical dialogue? What is the best way?

Chapter 6. As Disturbing Promise

1. How do you feel about the statement that the church ought to be a place or a community that disturbs us? Why?

2. What aspects of contemporary life do you think have the most significance for the church? How should the church change to meet the needs of people? How should it try to change the people so they can relate to the church more easily?

3. How do you think the changing roles of women in our society will affect the church? What are the issues surrounding women in the priesthood or ministry?

4. Most of Christian history draws upon the legacy of Western civilization. How will the church develop in non-Western areas? How should the American churches

respond to new immigrant and ethnic populations?

5. How do you think the church should get involved in public issues such as racial justice or nuclear disarmament? What is your reaction to a sermon that takes a political stand?

6. What is the relationship between religion and science? Should the church be concerned about ecology issues and medical advancements? Why?

7. Discuss the statement, "If the Good News that is Bad News breaks through a hardness of heart and occasions repentance, the Good News for the weak that comes as Bad News for the strong then becomes Good News for all." What is this difficult good news to you? Do you believe that you are part of any problem? Why?

8. How do we keep ourselves from becoming numb and insensitive to human need? More importantly, what is a Christian response?

9. Christians need to understand the place of the church in the world, the relationship of economics to the gospel, and the importance of worship. To what extent do you agree and disagree with this statement? What other things should concern contemporary church members?

SUGGESTIONS FOR FURTHER READING

Chapter 1. WITHIN POPULAR CULTURE

Furay, Conal. *The Grass Roots Mind in America.* New Viewpoints, Franklin Watts, 1977.

Nelson, John Wiley. *Your God Is Alive and Well and Appearing in Popular Culture.* Westminster Press, 1976.

Rauff, Edward A. *Why People Join the Church.* Pilgrim Press, 1979.

Stark, Rodney, and Glock, Charles Y. *American Piety: The Nature of Religious Commitment.* University of California Press, 1968.

Winter, Gibson. *The Suburban Capitivity of the Churches.* Macmillan Co., 1962.

Chapter 2. THROUGH PERSONAL TESTIMONY

Dudley, Carl. *Where Have All Our People Gone?* Pilgrim Press, 1979.

Hudson, Virginia Cary. *O Ye Jigs & Juleps!* Macmillan Co., 1962.

Kelley, Dean M. *Why Conservative Churches Are Growing.* Harper & Row, 1972.

Marty, Martin E. *A Nation of Behavers*. University of Chicago Press, 1976.

Rauff, Edward A. *Why People Join the Church*. Pilgrim Press, 1979.

Wagner, C. Peter. *Your Church Can Grow*. Regal Books, 1976.

Chapter 3. WITHIN BIBLICAL AND THEOLOGICAL TRADITIONS

Avis, Paul D. L. *The Church in the Theology of the Reformers*. John Knox Press, 1981.

Flew, R. Newton, ed. *The Nature of the Church*. London: SCM Press, 1952.

Huizinga, Johan. *Homo Ludens: A Study of the Play Element in Culture*. 1938. Reprint. Beacon Press, 1955.

Jay, Eric G. *The Church: Its Changing Image Through Twenty Centuries*. John Knox Press, 1980.

Küng, Hans. *The Church*. London: Sheed & Ward, 1967.

Minear, Paul S. *Images of the Church in the New Testament*. Westminster Press, 1960.

Niebuhr, H. Richard, and others. *The Purpose of the Church and Its Ministry*. Harper & Brothers, 1956.

Ramsey, A. M., and Suenens, Leon-Joseph. *The Future of the Christian Church*. London: SCM Press, 1971.

Schweizer, Eduard. *Church Order in the New Testament*. London: SCM Press, 1961.

Stewart, William. *The Nature and Calling of the Church*. Madras: Christian Literature Society, 1958.

Chapter 4. FROM HISTORICAL PERSPECTIVES

Ahlstrom, Sydney E. *A Religious History of the American People*. Yale University Press, 1972.

Bainton, Roland. *The Church of Our Fathers*. Charles Scribner's Sons, 1941.

Bowie, Walter Russell. *The Story of the Church*. Abingdon Press, 1955.

Day, Edward. *The Catholic Church Story: Changing and Changeless*. Liguori Publications, 1978.

Jay, Eric G. *The Church: Its Changing Image Through Twenty Centuries*. John Knox Press, 1980.

Marty, Martin E. *A Short History of Christianity*. Meridian Books, 1964.

Niebuhr, H. Richard. *Christ and Culture*. Harper & Brothers, 1951.

Rahner, Karl. *Concern for the Church*. Crossroad Publishing Co., 1981.

Ruether, Rosemary Radford. *The Church Against Itself*. Sheed & Ward, 1967.

Chapter 5. IN INSTITUTIONAL FORMS

Abbott, Walter M., ed. *The Documents of Vatican II*. Association Press, 1966.

Carroll, Jackson W.; Johnson, Douglas W.; and Marty, Martin E. *Religion in America: 1950 to the Present*. Harper & Row, 1979.

Fey, Harold E., ed. *A History of the Ecumenical Movement, 1948–1968*. Westminster Press, 1970.

Gaustad, Edwin Scott. *Historical Atlas of Religion in America*. Rev. ed. Harper & Row, 1976.

Gustafson, James M. *Treasure in Earthen Vessels*. University of Chicago Press, 1961.

Harrison, Paul M. *Authority and Power in the Free Church Tradition*. Princeton University Press, 1959.

In Quest of a Church of Christ Uniting. Consultation on Church Union, 1980.

Lincoln, C. Eric, ed. *The Black Experience in Religion*. Doubleday & Co., Anchor Press Book, 1974.

Neuhaus, Richard. *Freedom for Ministry*. Harper & Row, 1979.

Niebuhr, H. Richard. *The Social Sources of Denominationalism*. Meridian Books, 1957.

Richey, Russell E., ed. *Denominationalism*. Abingdon Press, 1977.

Rouse, Ruth, and Neill, Stephen Charles, eds. *A History of the Ecumenical Movement, 1517–1948*. Westminster Press, 1954.

Worley, Robert C. *A Gathering of Strangers*. Westminster Press, 1976.

Chapter 6. As DISTURBING PROMISE

Bonhoeffer, Dietrich. *The Cost of Discipleship*. 1959. Reprint. Macmillan Co., 1963.

_____. *Letters and Papers from Prison*. Macmillan Co., 1953.

Brown, Robert McAfee. *Frontiers for the Church Today*. Oxford University Press, 1973.

_____. *Is Faith Obsolete?* Westminster Press, 1974.

Dulles, Avery. *Models of the Church*. Doubleday & Co., 1974.

Hall, Douglas John. *Has the Church a Future?* Westminster Press, 1980.

McElvaney, William K. *Good News Is Bad News Is Good News . . . .* Orbis Books, 1980.

Rahner, Karl. *Concern for the Church*. Crossroad Publishing Co., 1981.

Ruether, Rosemary Radford. *Liberation Theology*. Paulist/Newman Press, 1972.

Schumacher, E. F. *Small Is Beautiful*. Harper & Row, 1975.

Soelle, Dorothee. *Death by Bread Alone*. Fortress Press, 1978.